DEVIL'S ADVOCATES

DEVIL'S ADVOCATES is a series of books devoted to exploring the classics of horror cinema. Contributors to the series come from the fields of teaching, academia, journalism and fiction, but all have one thing in common: a passion for the horror film and a desire to share it with the widest possible audience.

'The admirable Devil's Advocates series is not only essential – and fun – reading for the serious horror fan but should be set texts on any genre course.'
Dr Ian Hunter, Reader in Film Studies, De Montfort University, Leicester

'Auteur Publishing's new Devil's Advocates critiques on individual titles... offer bracingly fresh perspectives from passionate writers. The series will perfectly complement the BFI archive volumes.' **Christopher Fowler, *Independent on Sunday***

'Devil's Advocates has proven itself more than capable of producing impassioned, intelligent analyses of genre cinema... quickly becoming the go-to guys for intelligent, easily digestible film criticism.' ***Horror Talk.com***

'Auteur Publishing continue the good work of giving serious critical attention to significant horror films.' ***Black Static***

 DevilsAdvocatesbooks

DevilsAdBooks

DEVIL'S ADVOCATES

CRUISING

EUGENIO ERCOLANI &
MARCUS STIGLEGGER

ACKNOWLEDGEMENTS

The authors wish to express their thanks for help, discussion, and information to the following individuals:

John Atkinson, Nadine Demmler, Jack Fritscher, Buddy Giovinazzo, Dominik Graf, Lindsay Hallam, Jochen Hick, Marcus S. Kleiner, Ellen Manners, Adrian Martin, Kai Mihm, Shade Rupe, Amin Sabet, Danilo Vogt.

First published in 2020 by
Auteur, an imprint of
Liverpool University Press,
4 Cambridge Street,
Liverpool
L69 7ZU

Series design: Nikki Hamlett at Cassels Design
Set by Cassels Design www.casselsdesign.co.uk
Printed and bound by CPI Group (UK) Ltd, Croydon CR0 4YY

British Library Cataloguing-in-Publication Data
A catalogue record for this book is available from the British Library

ISBN paperback: 978-1-80034-808-0
ISBN hardback 978-1-80034-836-3
ISBN epub: 978-1-80034-772-4
ISBN PDF: 978-1-80034-607-9

CONTENTS

INTRODUCTION

It's a film about ambivalence. I thought the script read partly like Pinter, partly like Hitchcock, a whodunit, an adventure story. (Pacino quoted in Grobel 1979: 18)

When, on 2 August 1979, director William Friedkin left the gay bar the Cockpit in New York with his team and lead actor Al Pacino, bottles and angry chanting flew around their ears. Friedkin had hired hundreds of gay men as extras, many of whom were members of the leather scene, and more specifically its BDSM realm, to help him make his murder mystery Cruising as real as possible. Fuelled by articles in the weekly magazine Village Voice, gay male and lesbian activists mobilized against their counterparts and condemned them as 'traitors, sissies, and spoilsports'. In this atmosphere, Friedkin's team was under stress to finish shooting the controversial thriller, which has its foundation in an assortment of different sources, incidents, and coincidences.

It all starts with a severed arm found in the Hudson River. In the morgue, mysterious findings of a similar kind begin to raise questions: is a serial killer on the loose in New York? The gay leather scene of Manhattan has been terrorized by a series of brutal stabbings, and the sadistic offender seems to come from within the same subculture. The inexperienced patrolman Steve Burns (Al Pacino) is assigned to dive into the scene and play the decoy, since he physically resembles the murder victims. He accepts the unusual job hoping for a career jump; otherwise, he is uneasy about his assignment as he visits West Village bars like the Eagle's Nest, the Ramrod, and the Cockpit. For the heterosexual Burns, a journey into an unknown world begins which unsettles him regarding his sexual identity and affects his relationship with girlfriend Nancy (Karen Allen). While undercover, a friendship begins between him and his gay neighbour, Ted Bailey (Don Scardino), which later leads to an altercation involving Ted's boyfriend, Gregory (James Remar). A first suspect, Skip Lee (Jay Acovone), who is intimidated and beaten during an interrogation, turns out to be innocent, and Burns, outraged by the brutality and contempt the police have for the gay suspect, threatens to quit. However, his superior, Captain Edelson (Paul Sorvino), persuades him to keep going by motivating him with the prospect of a promotion to detective. Eventually, Burns appears to have identified the suspected killer: a Columbia University theatre student with schizophrenia named Stuart Richards (Richard Cox). After being propositioned by Burns one night in

Morningside Park, Richards turns on the policeman, attacking him, and is ultimately taken into custody. The police compare the student's fingerprints with those left by the killer in a sex cinema and they match, leading the case to be closed and Burns able to return to his girlfriend having been promoted to detective. Shortly after, Edelson is called to a crime scene, one in which he finds Ted stabbed to death. While there he discovers that Ted's neighbour, who has recently left his apartment, was named John Forbes: Burns' undercover alias. As Burns shaves in the bathroom in the final scene, Nancy tries on his leather clothes—a peaked cap, mirrored shades, and a squeaking, leather jacket—while her boyfriend looks at himself in the mirror. The last frame shows the Hudson River again where soon new body parts might turn up.

When *Cruising* was shown at the Berlin International Film Festival and hit cinemas worldwide in 1980 it was mainly misunderstood: the upcoming gay scene dismissed it as an offence to their efforts to open up to society and a distorted image of homosexuality. The distributors soon added a disclaimer that preceded the picture: 'This film is not intended as an indictment of the homosexual world. It is set in one small segment of that world, which is not meant to be representative of the whole.' Genre audiences were confused about the idea of a sexualized cop thriller with procedural drama that frequently turns into a horror film with the identity of the killer changing with each murder. Viewed as a generic slasher flick of its time—amidst the success of such films as *Halloween* (1978), *Friday the 13th* (1980), and *Maniac* (1980)—*Cruising* was too twisted and perverse (Schoell 1988: 64; Newman 1988: 102). Seen from today's perspective, Friedkin's film turned out to be an enduring cult classic documenting the gay leather scene of the late 1970s as well as providing a stunning image of identity crisis and an examination of male sexuality in general. In the fading years of the New Hollywood era (1967–1976), William Friedkin—the 'New Hollywood Wunderkind', with an Academy Award for his cop drama, *The French Connection* (1971), and following the tremendous success of his horror film, *The Exorcist* (1973)—proves once more the strength of his unique approach in combining genre and auteur cinema to create a fascinating film that turns 40 in 2020.

This book will dive deep into the phenomenon that is *Cruising*: it will examine its creative context and its protagonists, as well as explaining its ongoing popularity. Follow us on a journey into the dark rooms of this urban nightmare.

MEATPACKING DISTRICT: LIGHT AND DARKNESS AMONG THE RUINS

There's probably more leather sound than you'll ever hear in a film again.
(Paul Huntsman quoted in Segaloff 1990: 209)

Long stretching shadows on brick walls; pockmarked faces tinged with the faded colours of pulsating neon-lit signs; alleys vibrating to the sound of footsteps and metal chains; rivers of wet asphalt that become moats surrounding the Meatpacking District; and humid paths that cut through the damp soil of a darkened Central Park, its bushes and small bridges remaining as seemingly still as the dark water that presses against the edges of a contrasted Manhattan. The world of *Cruising*—the city of New York and the people within it—is a striking one, distinctive in its rhythm, its colour schemes, its sounds: in all the elements of what we could define as a realistic dream that nonetheless harbours a calm but menacing streak that gradually burns its borders and causes it to trickle into nightmarish territories.

William Friedkin puts on screen the flipside of a meticulously researched reality, twitching under the surface with nervous anticipation. As with nearly all of the director's best efforts, or most interesting films, the angles, shades, and gradations of the visual framework become the representation not only of a single macro-concept that encapsulates the story and its geographical and topographical context, but more importantly, the inevitable texture of the protagonist's psyche and state of mind. Because of Friedkin's capacity to permeate the look of his films with his characters' moods, paraphilias, and emotional inclinations, they tend to have a striking clarity, an immediacy to them. His films are articulated snapshots in which the psychological dimension and the mutations of the exterior are engaged in a continuous dialogue, and as often happens when we wake from dreams we exit the experience with one strong gut feeling that dominates whatever intellectual theory is trying to take shape within us. This visual–emotional implication means his films easily lend themselves to metaphors for the historical periods in which they were made, with all their accompanying social, cultural, and political issues. We could say that if ever there was a director whose films have the power to become—at times unwillingly or unknowingly—emotional and conceptual manifestos of specific moments in time, that director would be William Friedkin.

To further and better explain this thesis, let's take as an example the element of counterfeiting present in another pungent crime film adaptation directed by Friedkin, *To Live and Die in L.A.* (1985). This is, on a basic level, the type of criminal activity around which the story revolves, but it later becomes indispensable as the keystone to interpreting the film's lead and the world he lives in. Everything appears to contain some kind of truth or reality but ultimately ends up revealing itself to be no more than an imitation of what it should be: relationships, emotions, and even more so, morality, are all as fake as the money that passes from hand to hand. The gritty, sunbathed, colourful, and overexcited Los Angeles presented in the film heightens and amplifies this sense of plasticized reality. Although many have noted in its bleak cynicism and dysfunctional morality play elements attributable to the cinema of the previous decade, the film inevitably becomes a fierce yet satirical representation of eighties imagery in which heroism becomes the emblem of self-destructiveness and justice turns into an alibi for self-righteous male egocentrism: a dark parable of an over-stylized, hedonistic, and self-centred decade. *Cruising*, similarly, could be read as a bitter farewell to the seventies and its cinema and industry. Friedkin has never been a director scared or indecisive when it comes to entering sordid, dark, or controversial territories, but he had never approached a story with such rough directness; never had he sketched a world so deprived of human care and emotion. The road that lead Friedkin to the cold, blue-tinged landscape of *Cruising* is one that is indissolubly tied to the short but career-changing string of box office disappointments and critical slating the director endured, that began with the high-concept and ambitious *Sorcerer* (1977).

William Friedkin around 1980 ç

Whatever the film, when talking about William Friedkin it is impossible to separate him from the filmic movement in which he flourished, subsequently helped shape, and ultimately accompanied to its demise. From 1967—thanks to such films as Norman Jewison's *In the Heat of the Night* (1967), Mike Nichols' *The Graduate* (1967), and Arthur Penn's *Bonnie and Clyde* (1967)—to the first years of the 1970s, the American studio system goes through a period of rebirth, the result of which has come to be known as 'New Hollywood' cinema. The general trend of these and subsequent films is that of a new and unprecedented freedom from worn out formulas, old conventions, and censorship, with an eye steadfastly fixed on the 'Old Continent'. The target is that of a younger audience, which represents the majority of the ticket holders, and is now enriched by a new freedom of expression resulting from more liberal laws passed by the Supreme Court, and by the abandonment of the antiquated Motion Picture Production Code on behalf of the film industry. New Hollywood utilizes various elements of the filmic language adopted by art-house European cinema. The most eloquent example, in this sense, would be the *Nouvelle Vague* with its flashbacks, false bridging shots, and original use of the 180-degree rule. Soon, American directors will internalize within their cinema all the tools of European masters (mostly French and Italian) in personal, rough, real stories centred around actual issues that are profoundly human. Directors like Bob Rafelson, Sam Peckinpah, Hal Ashby, Dennis Hopper, Robert Altman, Paul Schrader, Francis Ford Coppola, and Peter Bogdanovich are among those directors capable and willing to tread new territories, deconstructing the narrative templates of Classical Hollywood and reshaping its formats; freeing themselves from the sound stages of the studio system; and bringing cinema to the streets of the cities and the dusty landscapes of its most impoverished and forgotten areas, oozing with genuine Americana iconography. Directors become authors who tap into their own experiences, upbringings, and fears, while, in the best cases, becoming reflections of the country's social and political life: holding a mirror to its heart of darkness. Cinema becomes the way to interpret, digest, and survive the turmoil of its times.

William Friedkin, after the release of his first feature-length film with what he has often defined as an 'awful mess'—the Cher–Sonny Bono musical comedy, *Good Times* (1967)—will embrace the opportunity, and after a triptych of small but well-conceived and critically acclaimed independent films (*The Birthday Party*, *The Night They Raided*

Minsky's, The Boys in the Band), he will reach the pinnacle of success with *The French Connection* (1971). The clashing of egos, the unwillingness to compromise, and the at times fierce competitiveness of this new breed of directors is part of celluloid mythology, and it has become impossible to separate legend from fact. If we take for granted many of the stories that have been circulating about this unique moment in Hollywood history, and believe unquestioningly Peter Biskind's *Easy Riders, Raging Bulls* (1998), then in this Olympus of gods and demons Friedkin would undoubtably be considered one of the latter. With two major box office hits under his belt, the second being, of course, *The Exorcist* (1973), Friedkin was truly a force to be reckoned with in Hollywood. Arrogant, confrontational, and authoritarian: the portrait that has survived of Friedkin in his most fervid period is one in which disorderliness and genial inclination meet. One of the many legends describes him as being so fiercely determined as to go to South America to bring *Sorcerer* to the screen upon discovering that his biggest rival and ex-partner in the Directors Company was going to the Philippines to shoot *Apocalypse Now* (1979).

According to Friedkin, the idea for the Directors Company came from Charles Bludhorn. Bludhorn, at the time chairman of the Gulf and Western Corporation which owned Paramount, made the deal without informing Frank Yablans, the studio's President, who was, unsurprisingly, strongly opposed to the idea of uniting the studio with the three notably difficult directors, Friedkin, Coppola, and the third but fundamental partner, Peter Bogdanovich, even though they were all making box office hits. Despite doubts along the corporate ladder, the birth of the company was announced. The initial agreement was for three films, each under $3 million: *Paper Moon* (Bogdanovich), *The Conversation* (Coppola), and *The Bunker Hill Boys* (Friedkin). The newly founded company got off to a strong start with the release of *Paper Moon* (1973), which was a critical and commercial success, followed by *The Conversation* (1974), which, despite being admired by the critical intelligentsia, performed less than moderately at the box office. The subsequent Bogdanovich-directed *Daisy Miller* (1974) flopped even harder, meaning Friedkin never managed to direct his film. In more recent years he has stated he was proud to be associated with *Paper Moon*, but did not like Coppola's effort, thinking it was a rip-off of Antonioni's *Blow-Up* (1966). He also says he was strongly opposed to *Daisy Miller* as he believed it wasn't commercial enough and felt its creation had been encouraged by Yablans partly in an attempt to end the collaboration between them and Paramount. The financial failure of its last film and the internal disagreements and divisions about *The Conversation* ultimately led to the company's demise. Friedkin claims another contributing factor was the tension created as a result of the adversarial position he took against Bogdanovich over *Daisy Miller*. Peter Bart, key executive within Paramount and subsequently vice president in charge of production, has often gone on record speaking of this period, but seems to have best summarized its difficulties in his 2004 article entitled 'Three's Company', published by *Variety*: 'The chief problem … was that it was never really a company. The three film-makers involved in its founding … relished the basic precepts of the enterprise, but, as true '70s mavericks, resisted serious involvement in its operation … Which was a shame because, had the company survived, these three (and other) film-makers had much to gain from it. All three of the founding film-makers went on to display rather arcane choices in material for their next films. All could have benefited from a collegial give and take with their peers.' The reasons behind the end of the 'generation that saved Hollywood' are many, but it is impossible not to highlight the failure of the Directors Company as a crucial watershed: the beginning of the end of a possibly utopian yet glorious dream.

The tale has been told within the pages of the abovementioned Biskind bestseller (1998: 337): the conversation between a visibly incredulous and increasingly nervous William Friedkin and the manager of the historic TCL Chinese Theatre of Los Angeles, while Friedkin's new wife, French actress Jeanne Moreau, witnesses the exchange in silence. *Sorcerer* was Friedkin's first feature since *The Exorcist*, released four years earlier, and the Bud Smith-cut trailer was being shown before none other than *Star Wars* (1977) as the conversation took place, a week before the second adaptation of Georges Arnaud's 1950 French novel, *Le Salaire de la peur*, was supposed to premiere in the famous Hollywood landmark. William Friedkin's film—which has been superficially but widely considered a remake of the 1953 film, *The Wages of Fear,* directed by Henri-Georges Clouzot—did in fact hit theatres shortly after and was completely annihilated by George Lucas's naïve, family-friendly space opera. *Sorcerer* was a life-changing disaster for Friedkin, managing to only bring in a miserable $9 million worldwide at the box office; thus, making it one of the most talked about and crucial financial failures of the decade, and one that would cement and definitively redirect Friedkin's career. One of the most ambitious of American cinema, the *enfant terrible*—in fact one of the main directors at the forefront of the Hollywood revolution—had reached his artistic breaking point, probably too blinded by his successes and the consequent contractual power bestowed upon him to realize that the audiences that had flocked to see *The French Connection* had irreversibly changed.

The difficulties surrounding the making of *Sorcerer* have been amply historicized and they mostly have to do with the continuous clashes between the director and the film's star, Roy Scheider, following a complex casting process which saw most of Friedkin's first choices declining the offer, the most notable example being Steve McQueen, who was willing to accept on the condition that a part be found for his then-partner, Ali MacGraw—something Friedkin was not willing to do. The ever-increasing budget, the hostile climate, and the technical difficulties for the long and complex sequences are just the glazing of the making of what will many years later be held as a cult classic, but for the first few years of its life the film was the largest and darkest ink stain on Friedkin's filmography. But drama has always seemed to take a shine to the Chicago-born director and more problems will riddle the production of his subsequent film, *The Brink's Job* (1978). During principal photography, a number of conflicts and concerns with the Teamsters union members occurred, ultimately resulting in four indictments and two convictions for attempts to solicit non-existent jobs. The film was initially developed by director John Frankenheimer, but after he pulled out producer Dino De Laurentiis passed the ball to Friedkin, who was looking for work after realizing that studios were no longer interested in any more of his own, more personal projects (among which was an adaptation of Ron Kovic's autobiography, *Born on the Fourth of July* (1976), a film that was ironically supposed to star actor Al Pacino). The script was completely rewritten by the director himself and Walon Green, who had partnered with Friedkin during the writing process of *Sorcerer*. Despite an Academy Award nomination for Best Art Direction and some positive—albeit never overly enthusiastic—reviews, the film became another financial failure, earning $14.5 million at the box office compared to the $16.4 million that made up the budget. Friedkin, interviewed in 2013 by Bilge Ebiri for *Vulture* magazine, stated that *The Brink's Job* was the film that ended up the 'farthest' from what he had initially envisioned.

By the time William Friedkin reached the brink of the decade's dawn, little was left of that new wave of film-making, which for a moment had shaken the world so violently, and it's difficult not to superimpose the torturous and winding road that is the career of William Friedkin onto those brick walls, animated with the virile movements of leather shadows, the clinking of metal studs, and the heavy panting that disperses in the moist New York night: not only for the vivid anger that permeates the whole film, the bruised eyes with which Friedkin seems to watch, to scrutinize his human fauna, but first and foremost for the lack of direction they all seem to have. None of the characters is a holder of certainties—only doubts. All are scattered, frightened souls surviving in a confused world, lacking or questioning their function, or their role, and going through the motions with mechanical convictions. *Cruising* also contains many of the narrative elements that Friedkin's audiences have come to expect from him, a substantial amount of which are connections with his previous films. An obvious comparison would be to *The Boys in the Band* (1970), given the theme of homosexuality, but additionally for the concept of a violent, dysfunctional police force: at times presented to us more like a Masonic underworld than as the upholders of the law, this is an idea also very much present in *The French Connection*. The lack of drive of Paul Sorvino's Captain Edelson could be compared to the wavering faith of Father Karras in *The Exorcist*, while the premise of someone accepting a difficult mission in dangerous and unknown territories can also be identified in the plot of *Sorcerer*. We can add to this list a very marked visual, experimental tone that accompanies the whole film, and a general grittiness we are used to associating with the director's best efforts and, more generally speaking, the films of the late sixties and early seventies. Rarely does a film act so perfectly as a junction between decades—the swansong, in this case hoarse and weakening, of a period in its twilight years.

Al Pacino starts, as the poster's tag line reads, 'cruising for a killer' on 28 October 1980. Undoubtedly, traces (at times striking ones) were still present of what had been— Martin Scorsese's seminal *Raging Bull* (1980) will be unleashed to audiences shortly after Friedkin's dark tale—but the American filmic landscape had profoundly changed, and *Cruising* finds itself squashed among rising trends and consolidating fashions. 1980 was a pivotal year (and in this first case, ironically) for knife-wielding, serial-killing, body-counting slashers (*Friday the 13th*, *Terror Train*, and *Prom Night*); for the shaping of what will later become known as the 'blockbuster' (*Flash Gordon* and, of course, the first sequel to the film that had changed so much for Friedkin, *The Empire Strikes Back*); and a new breed of comedy starring, more often than not, comedians born on the small screen at the time (*Caddyshack*, *The Blues Brothers*, *Seems Like Old Times*). *Cruising* didn't stand a chance, and if a romantic or sentimental view can be forgiven, then one might want to think back to the image of William Friedkin standing in the lobby of the TCL Chinese Theatre next to wife Jeanne Moreau—the two will divorce after barely three years of marriage in 1979, shortly before the making of *Cruising*—as the manager lists the box office figures for *Star Wars*.

(E.E.)

REALITY AND FICTION: THE BIRTH OF *CRUISING*

I never made the film to have anything to do with the gay community other than as a background for a murder mystery. It was not meant to be pro or con, gay rights, or gay anything. It was an exotic background that people, I knew, hadn't seen in a mainstream film. (William Friedkin quoted in Simon 1997)

The real story of *Cruising* begins in 1962 (also see Segaloff 1990: 192 ff.; Clagett 1990: 190 ff.). At the time, reports that a series of threats had been made against the homosexual community had filled the atmosphere of the still very secretive gay leather subculture in New York with fear. Two men, one black and one white, who became notorious as 'Salt and Pepper', would make their way around the West Village piers—a place where gay men commonly met back then. When they discovered people in flagrante, they would take photos and blackmail the victims. At least two of the blackmailed men were later found dead in their apartments. At the beginning of *Cruising* we see two cops on patrol (Joe Spinell and Mike Starr), passing by the Meatpacking District. In a dark alleyway they arrest two leather-clad cross-dressers and force them into their patrol car, where they begin to harass and threaten them. Friedkin varies his stories around those of Salt and Pepper, who at one point were themselves suspected to be two cops (an assumption that could never be confirmed). Hunting the real Salt and Pepper, the New York City Police Department (NYPD) decided to send one of their men, young cop Randy Jurgensen, undercover in the community of this gay subculture. He rented a flat in the area, researched the habits of those that were members of the scene, and began dressing and behaving like them. In the various clubs he was supposed to act as bait for the killer, or killers. Jurgensen was forced to keep his new identity a secret, making his reports directly with his captain, either by telephone or in person. He recalls that he wore tight denim pants, a black leather jacket, heavy boots, and studded bracelets, and painted his eyes darker. He had to adapt to a particular way of moving and talking in order to become part of the scene and went to sex shops to learn about the various codes that were commonly used there—a key example being the handkerchief code that signalled certain sexual preferences. Many such memories of Jurgensen's were later directly adopted by Friedkin and Pacino when making the film.

Al Pacino and Randy Jurgensen (© Lorimar/Warner Bros.)

Jurgensen basically worked alone, except when an arrest was going to be arranged. One evening he picked up a violent young man who they suspected could be the serial killer. Jurgensen wore a hidden microphone under his clothing and went with the suspect into a hotel in the Meatpacking District. His colleague, Sonny Grosso, and some other police officers had followed him and were waiting outside the hotel. However, when the connection to the microphone suddenly failed, Grosso entered the hotel in a panic. They found Jurgensen half-naked but unharmed with the suspect. This action led to the arrest of the young man, who was later found guilty of several misdemeanours, though it could never be confirmed whether he was the killer.

Jurgensen remembers that these activities had a huge impact on his personal life and gradually changed his identity. He made many friends within the subculture and began to identify with their needs and fears. When he was arrested, he had to stay in character and was repeatedly beaten by a huge, naked cop in a cowboy hat and a jockstrap—a scene later recreated for the film. What to audiences seems confusing and is refused an explanation in the film was a strategy to bring the suspect to breaking point. A similar scene appears in *The French Connection*, when 'Popeye' Doyle (Gene Hackman) asks a terrified suspect if he had 'picked his feet at Poughkeepsie': a strategy employed to confuse the man. At the same time Jurgensen became estranged from his family, and his private life was reduced to a minimum to protect the people close to him. The situation peaked in an incident when he was walking down Christopher Street arm in arm with two gay fellows and his wife's brother recognized him. Jurgensen was not able to fully explain this strange situation.

"The Exorcist"

Paul Bateson in The Exorcist (© Lorimar/Warner Bros.)

Events that happened over the course of two decades were written into the screenplay and told in a way that was as true as possible to the actual memories of Jurgensen, who was also a technical consultant on the film. He and his former partner, Sonny Grosso—another original 'French Connection cop'—were cast in Cruising as the detectives Lefransky and Blasio. Thus, Friedkin continued to embrace the semi-documentary tradition of his landmark crime flick, The French Connection, and deliberately mixed fact and fiction for maximum impact. This approach to work eventually seemed to take on a life of its own when Friedkin discovered that one of the extras in The Exorcist, a young medical assistant named Paul Bateson, was suspected to have committed the abovementioned murders. As he recalls in 2007: 'The assistant was later accused of a couple of the murders in the bars. I saw his picture in the papers and I got in touch with his lawyer, who arranged for me to meet with him at Rikers Island Penitentiary. I asked him what happened, and he told me. He also told me the police had offered him a better deal if he confessed to eight or nine of the murders, whether he'd done them or not. And I put that line in the film, because I found it so horrifying. I found out that he got out of prison three years ago, which means he got 25 years for what I took to be multiple murders' (Simon 2007).

Inspiration from real events aside, the basic plot of *Cruising* is drawn from that of a novel by Gerald Walker, who elaborated upon the series of unexplained murders of gay men in the early 1960s. Walker (1928–2004) was an articles editor for the *New York Times Magazine* from 1963 to 1990. In 1970 he published the novel *Cruising* about a young policeman, John Lynch, who, under the instruction of his superior, Captain Edelson, is searching undercover for an apparently gay serial killer. The killer turns out to be inconspicuous college student, Stuart Richards, who castrates some men in a sauna club and stuffs their genitals in their mouths out of pure self-loathing for his own homosexuality. The cop succeeds in stopping the offender, but when another man, Wally, with whom he had his first same-sex experiences, is killed, the investigator himself appears to have become a murderer. In his novel, the author equips his characters with extreme violence as the weapon with which to fight their own latent homosexuality. However, he does not even remotely begin to examine the gay community's perspective, including its resentment towards American society as a result of the social and religious moral pressures applied by the latter. Walker here characterizes gay men as being totally different from what he sees as average, urban people. While the novel might not be intentionally homophobic, it is clearly dated in its depiction of the gay underground. Wally is the only person characterized in a purely positive way here, while Lynch seems ambiguous with a back story of insecure masculinity. Nathan Lee writes in the *Village Voice* (2007): 'It's unclear whether or not Walker was aware of Jurgensen's operation, but the plot of his book is strikingly similar: A rookie NYPD cop goes undercover to bait a homophobic serial killer. Friedkin departs from Walker in manners large (shifting the point of view entirely to the cop) and small (changing his name from John Lynch to Steve Burns) while retaining details as specific as the subject of the killer's Columbia University thesis (the roots of the classic American musical—so gay! so evil!).'

William Friedkin (Simon 2007) remembers that at first, in the early 1970s, he was not even interested in the book:

I was offered the book *Cruising* by Gerald Walker to direct as a film, by Phil D'Antoni, who had produced *The French Connection*. I read the book and didn't think much of it. It was sort of interesting but I wasn't compelled to make it into a film at that time. Then Phil went out and got Steven Spielberg interested in making the film. And the two of them tried to get it set up for quite some time, and weren't able to. And D'Antoni is a great producer, really tenacious. We were turned down on *The French Connection* by every studio twice until Fox made it. But they finally gave up on *Cruising*. Three or four years later, Jerry Weintraub brought it to me, and said 'I heard you were interested in this, which is why I bought it. I want to do it with you.' I said 'Jerry, I wasn't interested in it. In fact, I turned it down with Phil.' He said 'Read it again. I think it would be a hell of a film.' Jerry's a very persuasive guy, but I still wasn't interested. Then several things happened: there were a series of unsolved killings in New York in the leather bars on the lower west side. The mysterious deaths that were taking place in the gay community, that later turned out to be AIDS, but really didn't have a name then. And the fact that my friend Randy Jurgensen, of the New York police department, had been assigned to go undercover into some of the bars, because he resembled some of the victims.

This way Friedkin cautiously connects the real-life story of Jurgensen with the semi-fictional events from Walker's novel.

It was the *Village Voice* columnist Arthur Bell himself (the author of the article that covered the murders Friedkin refers to) who called for a boycott of the film in a piece dated 16 July 1979, and in which he demanded the production be obstructed wherever possible (Schoell 1988: 61). This inspired protests during filming and the film launch in the US. Throughout the summer of 1979, a large and vocal segment of New York's gay community rallied to protest the production of a movie that seemed to—yet again—equate homosexuality with criminal insanity. Friedkin's film, in Bell's words, 'promises to be the most oppressive, ugly, bigoted look at homosexuality ever presented on the screen' (Lee 2007). Dedicated readers took to Greenwich Village rooftops, pointing mirrors at the set to interfere with the lighting, and surrounded it, blasting whistles and air horns. The most resourceful found out which apartments Friedkin would be using and set up in adjacent units to blast stereos. The owners of Christopher Street bars refused shooting permits for Friedkin and his crew. As Friedkin remembers:

Really the gay community was split. There were people who did not want shown anything that would present the gay community in anything but a good light, because the struggle for gay rights was in its very early stages then (1980). And I could see where the leaders of a certain element of the community would find this abhorrent because it wasn't showing the image of gays that they were promoting. On the other hand, there were a great many gays who saw the film who knew and understood that world and felt it was honest to that. (Simon 1997)

Protests during the shooting of Cruising *(© Lorimar/Warner Bros.)*

The protests against the shooting of *Cruising* could be seen as a foreshadowing of today's identity politics. The main argument against the film today would be that it was not made by gay men, but by straight people exploiting the subcultural scenery as an unfamiliar and exciting new backdrop for a simple murder mystery, and the director himself would appear to give this criticism weight by underlining that the subculture 'was an exotic background that people, I knew, hadn't seen in a mainstream film' (Simon 1997). When in one scene Al Pacino had to leave a building in Jones Street and was heading towards Bleecker Street, tenants of the building obstructed the shoot in a three-hour protest. They blocked the entrance and as soon as Pacino appeared, they jumped into the frame and aped his activities. In the evening, nearly four hundred protesters gathered in front of the Washington Square Methodist Episcopal Church and discussed further actions. The crowd grew fast and over three hundred people had to be sent home. By the end, shouting of the slogan 'gay power' could be heard. Arthur Bell commented on the effect of his initial article to Janet Maslin: 'What the Declaration of Independence was to Jefferson, that column was to the gay community' (Lee 2007). The production company and New York City officials denied their support of the protest, pointing towards the civil right of freedom of speech which protected the arts in particular.

Just before *Cruising* was ready to be released, another film featuring a controversial representation of homosexuality hit cinemas: *Windows* (1980) by Gordon Willis, an erotic thriller starring Talia Shire. The double provocation of *Cruising* and *Windows* fuelled protests within the gay community once again (which campaigned to 'stop the movies *Cruising* and *Windows*'); however, both films were ultimately failures at the US box office, and so the protests disappeared (Schoell 1988, pp. 63-65). Another similar protest occurred when *The Silence of the Lambs* (1991) by Jonathan Demme was released: the cross-dressing serial killer 'Buffalo Bill' (Ted Levine) was seen as a discrimination of transgender people in general. But this time the formula worked, and the film took in $273 million at the box office, earning a much-deserved string of Oscars, among which the one for Best Motion Picture in 1992.

As mentioned before, Steven Spielberg had been interested in an adaptation of Walker's novel long before Friedkin agreed to do it, but so too had Brian De Palma, who proposed a scene in which the killer murders a woman to confuse the investigators. After his departure from the project, De Palma went on to make his psychological thriller *Dressed to Kill* (1980), a film which could be called a 'global giallo': an international take on the Italian erotic thriller from the 1970s (Stiglegger 2018: 133–144). Michael Caine plays a transgender serial killer in New York. A variation on the undercover operation scene that revolves around a hidden microphone can be seen in De Palma's next film (also bearing the marks of a 'global giallo') *Blow Out* (1981). Here John Travolta plays a sound designer who at one point assists the police. Steven Spielberg, on the other hand, never referred to *Cruising* again.

(M.S.)

INTO THE LABYRINTH: THE IMMERSIVE SOUNDSCAPES AND EERIE VOICES OF *CRUISING*

The *acousmêtre* in film conveys ubiquity, panopticism, omniscience, and omnipotence. (Chion 1999: 24)

Cruising's narrative structure is a deliberately fractured labyrinth. Images and sounds provide pieces of a puzzle, but one that will only ever be fully reconstructed within the confines of our own imaginations. From his early success with *The French Connection*, Friedkin's films move from event to event, from incident to incident, in an associative way, making it hard to group these scenes into the classic dramaturgic three- or five-act structures. In *Cruising* it takes over 15 minutes for protagonist Steve Burns to enter the screen and, in the meantime, we are confronted with several significant side characters that we cannot be sure will reappear. Friedkin seems heavily inspired by a more European approach to *mise en scène* and montage, similar to that of Andrzej Żuławski, Ken Russell, or Henri-Georges Clouzot. This fragmented narration and associative montage along with his unusual sound design could be the reason for the disturbing effectiveness of his successful films (*The French Connection* and *The Exorcist*), but also the rejection of his initially marginalized works (*Sorcerer* and *Cruising*). It is not simply as a result of the controversy of the subject matter that incited the negative response to *Cruising*, but also the way in which the film's urban nightmare world is constructed: it is the style itself that takes us 'to the furthest reaches of disorientation and ambiguity', as Australian film critic Adrian Martin (2008) puts it. *Cruising*'s sound design is a document of pure horror—an aural experience in terror.

Cruising hints at narratives that are inconsistent with the murders that we witness on screen, and if we accept the *mise en scène* as the objective account of what happens we soon realize: *Cruising* takes place in a world of 'doppelgängers', of dark doubles. During each homicide the murderer switches either body, voice, or both: in one instance, the killer resembles a former (or possibly later) victim. Thus, Friedkin teaches us to not trust our visual perception: 'we are led to suspect, in one way or another, that virtually every character in the film could be the killer, potentially or actually, in the past, present, or future of the narrative' (Martin 2018). In addition, the disembodied voices used by the film resemble the demonic voices of the possessed in *The Exorcist*, where several people speak 'in tongues'. The following chapter will expand on and analyse how this distortion of visual perception is achieved within the film.

The severed arm in Hudson River (© Lorimar/Warner Bros.)

From the first scene, Friedkin defines a set of rules according to which the film and its soundtrack interact: droning electronic sounds, pulsing bass guitar, and mysterious bells accentuate the tristesse along the Hudson River. The sound dictates how we interpret the images and when a severed arm appears in the water, we know that it might be even worse than expected. In the morgue of the police station a detective and the coroner discuss a series of unsolved cases associated with various body parts. Again, the droning electronic score materializes, interweaving this scene with the night-time patrol of two policemen commenting on their marital problems and the gay leather subculture in the Meatpacking District of lower Manhattan. The soundtrack of *Cruising* was arranged by Jack Nitzsche, a pop and rock music producer who also composed the remarkable soundtrack of Nicolas Roeg and Donald Cammell's *Performance* (1970) and Friedkin's own *The Exorcist*. Nitzsche, compared to many of his contemporaries, was more of an experimental composer, and if you are listening to the original 3-LP set (2019) soundtrack of *Cruising* it becomes quite clear that some of the atmospheric electronic sections and ambiences draw on pieces composed by other musicians. At the beginning of the film Nitzsche mixes simple keyboard sounds with the more elaborate jazzy ambience created by Barre Phillips (from his album *Three Day Moon*). Friedkin likes to work with a lot of temporary tracks during the editing process—a fact that also led to the omission of Lalo Schifrin's original soundtrack recordings for *The Exorcist* some years before, when the director refused to remove the track 'Tubular Bells' by Mike Oldfield from the film. *The Exorcist* was scored with experimental but already existing pieces of Neue Musik by Krzysztof Penderecki, Anton Webern, and Hans Werner Henze. In *Sorcerer*, Friedkin chose the German Krautrock pioneers of electronic music Tangerine Dream. For *Cruising* he combined these styles and added plenty of contemporary punk and hard rock songs. Thus, among these films, *Cruising* has the most complex sound and music design (equalled only by his later cop thriller *To Live and Die in L.A.*).

As previously examined, the filming of *Cruising* was troubled by heavy protests which made it virtually impossible to use the actual location sound recordings. As a result, nearly 80 per cent of the film was dubbed and rescored, which led to several parts of the film's final sound design coming about by accident and varying from how they were originally intended. However, Friedkin used this opportunity to his advantage, pushing the design and stylization of the soundtrack to the then-known limits. This meant reducing the location ambience and focusing on singular noises; mixing several new and known musical sources to create genuine soundscapes; layering songs; using dubbed voices and syncing them with various actors; and deliberately confusing non-diegetic and diegetic sound elements. The use of location sound recording did not begin with early sound film but much later. In the 1930s, sound was used selectively and mainly diegetically (motivated within the frame), with the exception of any non-diegetic music or off-screen narration. In the Classical Hollywood of the 1950s, atmospheric sound was well established, but its omission was frequently used as a meaningful stylistic choice, such as in the final scene of *Psycho* (1960) where we find Norman Bates (Anthony Perkins) trapped in his own mind. Especially the cinema of the New Hollywood era was known for experimenting with classical sound conventions. From Dennis Hopper to Friedkin himself not only was popular music employed but also hyperreal sounds, used in an isolated way. This technique is used in the final scene of *The French Connection*, where we hear the sound of water drops after 'Popeye' Doyle's accidental killing of his colleague.

The killer enters the Cockpit during the last act of Cruising *(© Lorimar/Warner Bros.)*

Whoever has seen *Cruising* will never forget the sound of clanging keys fixed to the leather belt of the fetish uniform, engineer boots hitting asphalt, and the squeaking leather of the Langlitz and Schott Perfecto jackets seen in the club and bar scenes. While redubbing the film, Friedkin included these hyperreal but isolated, iconic sounds that have become unique to it. The scene towards the beginning of the film, where a leatherman (Larry Atlas) enters the basement bar the Cockpit, is accompanied by this soundscape of fetish noises, and it is exactly this shot of the killer (at the Hotel St. James) that appears again towards the end of the film, when, having been confronted with Ted's murdered body, Edelson realises that the case may not in fact be closed. Here, the former victim from the park can be interpreted as the killer entering the Cockpit (again). Thus, a new cycle of death and mayhem begins. The Hotel St. James scene is also dominated by the sound of leather squeaking, lustful breathing, and whispering, as well as the loud ticking of a clock. Friedkin refuses to dramatize the events with additional music—the sound themselves can be seen as a *musique concrète*. This hypnotic use of sound is combined with deliberately fragmented framing: we only ever see either the naked bodies of the two men or very close shots of the killer's face, his eyes covered by mirrored shades. After he has tied his victim (Arnaldo Santana) to the bed in a series of jump cuts, he holds the knife over the back of the helpless man and stabs him several times: 'I know what I have to do.'

The Hotel St. James murder scene (© Lorimar/Warner Bros.)

This violent close-up is intercut with the killer's face and split-second shots of male anal intercourse. These cuts are only a few frames long and can hardly be seen—a technique called subliminal editing and often used by Friedkin in his films during violent and shocking scenes. In all different versions of Cruising (cinema, VHS, DVD, Blu-ray) these hardcore cuts are coloured differently: from monochrome, to black and white, to a natural colour scheme in the current version, as if Friedkin was unsure if he wanted the viewer to actually see them or not. These close-ups are highly explicit and may give an indication of some of the sexually graphic material cut from the first version of the film.

As Adrian Martin (2018) points out, Cruising 'sets up a system in which different sorts of places or locations have their own distinctive sound, including their own kind of music.' In the police building we mainly have silence and an overemphasis of the dialogues and actual on-screen sounds (for example the bone saw in the morgue). When Steve Burns enters Greenwich Village, he moves into his apartment to the sound of eerie drones and disconnected noises. Later, he meets his gay neighbour in a coffee shop, in a scene supplemented by natural location recordings—as was the realistic tendency of many New Hollywood films of the 1970s. Diverse again are the accompanying soundtracks for the moments between Steve and Nancy. Here we have significant use of a classical string piece, 'Passa Calle (Allegro vivo)' by Luigi Boccherini, the most harmonic music of the film, though distorted with a subtle reverb effect. This track is played over the final scene in the bathroom as it fades into a shot of the Hudson River, until Willy DeVille's 'It's So Easy' brutally breaks in. The harmony of the former piece seems something of a façade waiting to be undermined at any moment.

When Friedkin visited the gay clubs of New York he realized that the music played there was mainly the disco sound of the late 1970s, covering the cliché of 'Y.M.C.A.' by the Village People. As the location sound was of no use, he asked Jack Nitzsche to bring along some pounding punk rock and funky guitar tracks. Friedkin also brought in Willy DeVille with 'Heat Of The Moment', 'It's So Easy', and 'Pullin' My String'; the Cripples with 'Loneliness' and 'Hypnotize'; John Hiatt with 'Spy Boy'; Rough Trade with 'Shakedown'; Mutiny with 'Lump'; and Madelynn von Ritz with 'When I Close My Eyes I See Blood'. Nitzsche also recorded a small set of songs with the later legendary punk band the Germs, but only 'Lion's Share' made it into the film's peep show scene. The extensive use of these rough rock songs in the club and street scenes of the film creates a unique atmosphere of aggressive sexuality, tension, and raw male energy. Just listening to the song-based soundtrack album brings to mind the sexually charged moments of the film which contribute to the latter's unique vision of the subculture—more of an interpretation of the gay leather scene than a true documentation.

William Friedkin is a master of cinematographic seduction and immersion. In his films the audience is never safe, and he leads us to places we never even dared fantasize about: the slums of the Bronx; the desert of Iraq; the South American jungle; and finally, the Meatpacking District of Manhattan. With all his directorial skills Friedkin lures us into another world full of contradictions, transgressions, and the abject. He forces us to confront things that are secretly part of us (as humans) but that we'd rather not look too closely at. His films transgress the borders of the morally acceptable in the eyes of mainstream culture and he establishes characters for us to identify with that are ambiguous about their own desires and abilities. This is what seduction in the context of film theory means (Stiglegger 2006): how can a fictional film manipulate us into diving into a world that we would avoid in our everyday lives? Friedkin's films ask the right questions from the beginning and leave us alone with them. We are left to deal with the fragments we get, while our secret desires may be triggered and exposed. Here, Friedkin's films go way beyond the artificial beauty of a Classical Hollywood film (such as Hitchcock's *Vertigo* (1958)). *Cruising* manages to create an abyssal aesthetic that makes New York look like a highly sexually charged Gotham City—not unlike how the city is presented in William Lustig's *Maniac* (1980) or Lucio Fulci's *Lo squartatore di New York* ('The New York Ripper', 1982). In its unique sound design the film has highly immersive potential: Friedkin manipulates the way in which we experience the strange world of 'aberrant' sexual desires through his use of drones, distorted noises, pounding rock beats, eerie voices, and confusing experimental pieces.

This method of seduction through immersion utilized in *Cruising* can be exemplified and subsequently examined in the park murder segment that features 'Spy Boy', a song written by John Hiatt and which refers to the voyeuristic nature of the cruising culture. We follow Eric (Larry Atlas, who played the killer in the Hotel St. James) on his way towards the park as he locks eyes with potential hook ups here and there, moments which the audience witnesses from his point of view. The slow, pulsing beat of the song provides the rhythm for the scene, and after inspecting a long line of men Eric's eventual

Burns and Edelson, Richards and his father – father/son relationships (© Lorimar/Warner Bros.)

choice is one hidden in darkness at the end—a man who is in fact college student Stuart Richards. The song is not played as loudly as a non-diegetic film track would normally be, but at a volume that makes it seem as though it could instead be being played live somewhere nearby, potentially also heard by the characters. As the young men enter the bushes in the park, the song fades and gives way to mysterious sounds and voices. We are forced into Eric's point of view as he becomes panicked, having lost sight of the object of his desire. Richards whispers, 'where are you? I'm waiting for you,' and thrusts his knife into Eric's back. Once again—and for the last time—we find ourselves seeing the world as Eric does, his shock and pain creating a distorted perception of reality. We see fragmented trees and hear a confusing mixture of sounds: a scream, traffic, and animal noises. In that moment, Friedkin merges us with the dying man, and we become Stuart Richards' victim. The image fades to black as Richards stabs once more. An unexpected cut brings us to a wide shot of Steve Burns in full leather attire walking along the street, 'Spy Boy' playing again in the background with a haunting reverb effect. This time Burns is not focused on hunting for the killer—the next shot shows him having sex with Nancy, as he grips the edge of the bed with his hand, his wrist still adorned with a leather bracelet. Shown in the wake of the act of ultraviolence we witness the aggressive mixing of two worlds: the bizarre and the 'profane'; sexualities that are obscured, and those that are overt.

An important aspect of the use of voice in Cruising is that of Stuart Richards' father: the mysteriously disembodied voice, the acousmêtre (Chion 1999: 24). It is this voice that seems to command the killings, and that constantly disturbs Richards. Its use ('You know what you have to do!') in some scenes recalls moments in Alfred Hitchcock's Psycho when Norman Bates takes on the voice of his mother. The idea of a negative parent figure is also illustrated in Steve Burns' reaction to his girlfriend's remark that his father called. Embodied is the father in the character of Edelson, who sends his 'son' Burns onto the streets of violence with the objective of restoring order to the system. As a dedicated viewer we work hard to ascertain exactly who it is that utters the crucial phrases repeated throughout the film ('You made me do that'; 'I am here, you are here...') and which hint towards the identity of the killer. Instead of clearing this uncertainty up towards the end of the film and definitively assigning voices to characters, Friedkin mixes the key expressions in their original versions with on-screen moments in which they are uttered, as he does when Burns finally confronts Richards in the park. It is never clear from where Burns learns the exact phrase, which to characters in the film other than the victims or the audience is only vaguely hinted at earlier on by one of the cross-dresser informers when they speak with Edelson. The fact that Steve Burns knows the words of the killer(s) makes him one of the suspects: a suspicion which is affirmed at the end when his former neighbour is found dead.

The confusing use of the 'disembodied voice' is another link between *Cruising* and the Italian giallo thriller. Especially in films by Dario Argento from 1970—*L'uccello dalle piume di cristallo* ('The Bird with the Crystal Plumage')—onwards, we hear whispered words that can be associated with the killer, hinting at their identity; however, the audience is often left in doubt about the actual source of or body belonging to the voice. Its discorporate nature makes it more frightening than if it were connected to a certain body, as this would create some clarity for the viewer. The use of such a voice in *Cruising* identifies the film as a 'global giallo thriller' (see the respective chapter in this book) and also gives it a shared characteristic with American slasher films that employ the terrorising 'voice without a body', an example of which being Wes Craven's *Scream* (1996), where the distorted voice is ultimately identified as a fabrication of the voices of two actual killers. In this example, the stereo effect of the sound design adds further immersive dimensions to the mystery. In *Cruising*, the mystery remains beyond the film's ending, and we will never know if Burns is one of the film's killers or just a deeply disturbed young cop with an identity crisis.

(M.S.)

WILLIAM FRIEDKIN'S 'INFERNAL TRILOGY': CONTEXTUALIZING *CRUISING*

If we wanted to explore the heart of William Friedkin's oeuvre, we could speak of two essential, personally motivated trilogies. The first encompasses *The French Connection* (1971), *The Exorcist* (1973), and *Sorcerer* (1977). This trilogy explores the idea of homosexuality in the context of several exceptional circumstances; we could call it the 'buddy trilogy'. The 1980s and 1990s are dominated by Friedkin's critical reflections on American society: *Cruising* (1980), *To Live and Die in L.A.* (1985), and *Jade* (1995) develop complex, allegorical models using a malicious, surgical approach. To contextualize *Cruising*, it is worth looking at this latter 'infernal trilogy', especially since these three films have so far received less respect than the previous ones. (Stiglegger 2000: 16–22)

As already illustrated, the horror thriller *Cruising* caused a sensation in the New York gay community in 1980 when William Friedkin staged his adaptation of Gerald Walker's novel as authentically as possible in the Greenwich Village leather scene. The protagonist, Steve Burns, alternates between his bourgeois–heterosexual relationship with girlfriend Nancy, and the darkly shimmering world of gay hypermasculinity, in which women ultimately seem to have no place. Several scenes suggest that the policeman gradually succumbs to this fascination with the morbid. He steels his body, carries the insignia of dominance—leather jacket, cap, motorcycle boots, chains—and is engaged in his function as a decoy in fast sex in a cheap hotel, where he is promptly interrupted by his colleagues. He becomes an outsider, wandering between worlds. His superior, Captain Edelson, remains his only—quite paternal—friend.

In *Cruising*, Friedkin tells of the thin line between ritualized and destructive violence. The initially stimulating 'psychodrama' of the sadomasochistic act flows seamlessly into a crime. *Cruising* was, at the time, underestimated as simply a slasher/horror thriller and was even dismissed as anti-gay. However, if one looks closely at the film, the following idea becomes evident: Friedkin makes use of the apocalyptic, 'modern primitive' charisma of the leather scene as an allegory. In muddy colours, with his usual sophistication, he visualizes the sexually bizarre world as a sideline to the violence-based, patriarchal American society. Although he is not exactly disrespectful to the gay community, and is principally motivated by fascination, we have to admit that the film can hardly do justice to a community that was, at that time, dealing with emancipatory needs. The meticulousness with which he photographs the club scenes of the pre-AIDS era, however, could hardly be more authentic. With Steve Burns, the viewer approaches first frightened, then fascinated, this death-related sexual 'limbo' that would be the nightmare of any American puritanical republican. *Cruising* is an attempt to turn an objectively narrated thriller plot into an apocalyptic horror scenario without using the striking special effects of horror cinema, and at the same time uncovering the dark underbelly of North American society.

Graffito in the French and Italian versions: 'We are everywhere', omitted from the US version (© Lorimar/ Warner Bros.)

Only five years after *Cruising*, Friedkin once again managed to create a personal exploration of the American dream. He begins with the nihilistic pop chords of band Wang Chung—an experimental soundtrack that oscillates between pounding rhythms and eerie ambient passages—with a blood-red, dawning sunrise over Los Angeles. The president is about to arrive; the American flag flaps in the wind as FBI agents secure a VIP hotel. President Ronald Reagan speaks to the news cameras. The rising young agent,

Chance (William L. Petersen), is suddenly alarmed: failing in his attempt to assassinate the president, a Palestinian kamikaze terrorist is blown to pieces by him over the roofs of the sparkling city. Chance's more experienced partner admits he feels 'too old for this shit'. The next day the older agent will be killed by ruthless counterfeiter Rick Masters (Willem Dafoe). While avenging the murder of his partner serves as Chance's apparent motivation in the events that follow, *To Live and Die in L.A.* only superficially unfolds this narrative. Instead, Friedkin's intent is to explore the state of the dusty, corrupt city of LA: a devastated, hate-ridden society; a fatal melting pot, just moments before the Rodney King riots. 'I can't get away / To live and die in LA', Wang Chung sing along in their alluring pop hit. In addition to the poison-green letters of the title, which are reminiscent of the mendacious neo-aesthetics of the then-popular police series, a bullet hits the picture: the drop of blood trickles down and forms a palm tree—the symbol of California.

Debra Feuer made-up in To Live and Die in L.A. *(© MGM/UA)*

In this second instalment of the 'infernal trilogy', the director is interested in complex personal constellations and transformations. FBI agent John Vukovich (John Pankow) becomes increasingly similar to his new death-driven partner, Chance, and ultimately replaces him in all aspects of his life, including in his relationship with extorted lover Ruth (Darlanne Fluegel). When the exceptionally cruel counterfeiter, Masters (a failed painter as we learn), visits his girlfriend Bianca (Debra Feuer) in her dressing room, she is considered a man until the short-haired wig releases her long red curls. Later, Masters will surprise her with a young female dancer as a lover/present, and the woman takes Masters' place after he is shot by Vukovich. In this world everyone is replaceable and will end up betraying one another out of the common instinct to survive, ultimately leading them to self-destruction (Clagett 1990: 245–246). Vukovich's final attempt to take over Chance's role, life, and function is depicted as a failure, seeing him become no more than a shallow imitation, and this is an idea that Friedkin seems to underline in a scene after the end credits finish rolling: the image of an intimidating Chance lingering in the shadows of his lover's bedroom. To show such a scene was an unusual move at a time when the credits were usually ignored by the audience. But Friedkin trusts in the *Gesamtkunstwerk*, the inseparable sum of the composition of exquisite ingredients. It is astonishing today that this successful 'action movie' was criticized at the time as 'the outgrowth of video clip production': even faster, even harder, even louder. Of course, he handles these attributes expertly, whether it be in the rapid hunts through the flood channels or against the traffic on the L.A. highway, or in the bloody shoot-outs in which almost all protagonists lose their lives. In a step further from *Cruising*, *To Live and Die in L.A.* is the essence of the police film of his time: the plot is hardly of interest—it is adapted from a somewhat crude thriller by Gerald Petievich—and Friedkin reflects the state of mind of his time in allegorical, sometimes exaggerated images of blundering violence. No longer the gloom and cold of *Cruising*'s New York, but the bright, hectic, visually stimulating atmosphere of the Californian metropolis pushes unpleasantly into the foreground. *Cruising* and *To Live and Die in L.A.* play on genre stereotypes, but are ultimately interested in an infernal portrait of society: labyrinthine, fragmented cities, dark and dusty; virulent, rampant violence; corrupt, interchangeable characters at all levels. Sexual extremism is as remote as Rick Master's Francis Bacon-oriented art, which he burns and destroys right at the beginning of the film.

Friedkin's films are complex, elusive at first sight. An unmistakable feature of his signature has become disturbing flashbacks or flash forwards. This destruction of linear time (which is a technique also employed in the films of Nicolas Roeg) raises questions that are explained late—often too late—in the plot and forces the audience to continuously reanalyse events in an attempt to comprehend them. Since *The Exorcist*, he has also repeatedly used subliminal images: frames of one twenty-fourth of a second in length, which the viewer can only perceive subconsciously, but which can nevertheless be identified. In *Cruising* and *To Live and Die in L.A.*, this technique is used in a wider sense when a nervous tension hijacks the perception of the protagonists. As Vukovich breaks down in the back seat of the car during the chase along the freeway, Chance's adrenaline fever is contrasted by a minimal cut to his earlier bungee jumping. Vukovich will later also be consumed by that adrenaline addiction as he kills Masters in a superhuman effort.

In his criticism of Friedkin's late work, especially *Jade*, Larry Gross wrote in the British film magazine *Sight & Sound* (December 1995): 'His main work was drastic, almost perverse personally.' The erotic thriller, *Jade*, written by Joe Eszterhas, seemed at first sight nothing more than a fashion trendsetter, one of the followers of Paul Verhoeven's *Basic Instinct* (1992), yet it fitted in neatly with the earlier portraits of 'deviant sexualities' in Friedkin's filmography. In San Francisco, an influential politician is brutally slain with an African artefact. Detective Corelli (David Caruso) suspects the psychologist Trina Gavin (Linda Fiorentino), who met the victim moments before his death. However, Trina's husband, the well-known lawyer Matt Gavin (Chazz Palminteri), protects her unconditionally. While the trail of the crime leads to the governor of California (Richard Crenna), who was blackmailed by the victim with sex photos, they are slowly becoming aware of the pitfalls of the constellation: Trina was once Corelli's mistress, but she chose his best friend Matt. Corelli is still succumbing to Trina, secretly seeking evidence of her innocence. Trina is simultaneously the secret prostitute Jade. Corelli notes that his investigations are being sabotaged from within his own ranks; a witness is murdered, and it becomes clear that Trina is to serve as a scapegoat. Of course, it's the governor who wants to keep suspicions about him at bay and allow Trina to be murdered. At the end Matt confesses to the first murder to Trina. In his last sentence he tells her: 'Next time we make love, you introduce me to Jade.'

Jade presents a conglomeration of Eszterhas' preferred plot fragments. It is clear from the beginning who the killer is (the lost cufflinks are proof), though the clue isn't as obvious as the one offered in *Basic Instinct*, which suggests that Catherine Tramell (Sharon Stone) may not be the killer. In the world of *Jade*, the protagonists are at the mercy of their desires and dreams—similar to *Cruising*, but in another milieu. They drift between lies and secrets. They are unable to use the rigorous rituals of *Cruising*'s leather scene for initiation, or surrender to the suicidal adrenaline rush of the FBI agents from *To Live and Die in L.A.* Consequently, it is another type of hunt that takes place in *Jade*: a circular one. A liberating width that exists in L.A. is missing in San Francisco. Violence is never successfully externalised but leads to implosion: the getaway car ploughs slowly through a Chinese New Year parade and leaves behind numerous injured—the winding roads of San Francisco are hardly suitable for linear movement. The hunts in *Jade* are halting, interrupted, characterized by calm rather than breathlessness. And the injuries are always clearly and devastatingly shown (an example being when Angie Everhart gets run over twice by a car).

A commercial project like *Jade* gives its director little freedom in dealing with the subject matter. But Friedkin has learned his trade. He flatters the action in incomparably stylish ways with a sliding camera, using Loreena McKennitt's ethereal, gothic song, 'The Mystic's Dream', as a hypnotic leitmotif, and even more so by creating blatantly contrasting highlights in the shock sequences. His staging of details, especially the African mask in the house of the first victim, achieves nightmarish qualities. Again, the director refuses a release from the free floating of desire in North American society. From the basements of New York, through the highways of L.A., to the villas of San Francisco, there is a brooding repression that pushes his characters to act in overtly violent ways—a new 'disease to death'. William Friedkin sadly holds the banner of Hollywood's new *fin de siècle*. His 'infernal trilogy' could be seen as a self-aware addition to the New Hollywood era of the glorious seventies. The age of experimentation and social awareness seems over. But Friedkin is aware of the generic images and clichés he uses. Quotation, intertextuality, and self-referentiality have become stylistic devices on which a new generation of film-makers are building their cinema of emotions. Within this context, Friedkin's trilogy stands out as a successful and acute attempt to expose American society and the film industry alike. The seed was planted with *Cruising* and may still be fruitful in Friedkin's later and smaller films. He never lost the sensibilities of 1970s socially aware cinema but had to find new means by which to expound the darkness and decay.

(M.S.)

IT'S A MAN'S WORLD: *CRUISING'S* HYPERMASCULINE UNIVERSE

Pacino arrived filled with enthusiasm but little knowledge of gay life, let alone S&M, and he didn't want to see the locations before filming. He wanted to experience them fresh as his character would. (Friedkin 2013: 367)

Cruising examines a patriarchal, or phallocratic, society, in which the power invested in men by the law expresses itself through a valorisation of male sexuality, the penis. (Martin 2018)

William Friedkin's camera moves, lingers on, and observes the masculine body with an intensity that oscillates between a descriptive, nearly anthropological eye, and a complacent, morbid clinginess. Muscles flexing in dark corners; tense sweat-drenched skin glistening under intermittent neon lights; naked, virile flesh bursting through tight strips of lucid leather outfits; damp chest hair and thick rough skin exposed to the eye with overbearing exhibitionism. The slow pan shots within the crowded clubs of *Cruising* show a shifting, ever-changing landscape of bodies: a sticky and damp world oozing with testosterone, choreographed to the rhythm of heavy panting and moaning, breaking through the mist of music and smoke. Leather creatures made of multiple arms and legs, pulsating with aggressive, palpitating desires.

The memory and images of *Cruising* that linger on in the audience's mind are that of a world permeated by a strong sense of masculinity: in fact, by its multifaceted nature in a continuous transition between mundane mainstream life and the party world enveloped within. From the buzzing streets of New York to the epicentre of one the darkest corners of its underbelly, we witness a metamorphosis of the characters not only in their change of clothing and the striking consequent chromatic contrast, but also in their language and behaviour. To *cruise* in Friedkin's film means to enter a parallel dimension with its own set of rules, and most importantly its own communicative code. Like in an over-stylized, night-drenched, post-apocalyptic landscape, what dominates is not social status: one's bank account, job, or reputation. In fact, these social parameters, together with names and surnames themselves, are redundant, meaningless dregs of personas momentarily abandoned in office cubicles, building sites, and crowded sidewalks. The neon lights and shadows of *Cruising*'s nightclubs have a levelling power; all men are the same—may they be crooked cops, students, or those coming from the upper echelons of the Manhattan intelligentsia—and as if in a somewhat Darwinian, dystopian aftermath, what counts is one's capacity to dominate in a given context, to possess the power of attraction, of physical dominance, and the manifestation of a strong sexual drive. The survival of the fittest, strongest, the most virile, the most persistent. A world made of action, not of words: of needs and desires, not of cerebral labyrinths.

Steve Burns enters the hypermasculine world (© Lorimar/Warner Bros.)

Most of what is being exposed here is perfectly exemplified in the character of fashion designer Martino Perry, played by actor Steve Inwood. Friedkin gives us a glimpse of his normal, mundane life: upper-class yet ordinary. Not interested in narrative exposure or backstory, Friedkin maintains an anthropological eye. We spy our subject as he moves and talks within his high-class Manhattan store, and exits accompanied by who is presumably his assistant, boxes in hand, towards his car. What we are supposed to pick up on is context, behaviour, the visible and incalculable wealth, and social position—and then witness the disappearance of all the above as the normality of the New York rush hour discolours into the turbid night. It's difficult not to see the act of some of the key characters (among which the film's lead) going down a ramp of stairs to enter the club as being metaphorical: the passage into the underworld, into the underground of a collective subconscious shared by members of a society beyond suspicion. Martino Perry rids himself of his social persona; the idea of that successful fashion designer giving instructions to his personal assistant as taxis honk in the background is one destined to last very little in the audience's mind. Perry visits an adult bookstore and follows someone—who we as the audience know is the serial killer—into a sticky-looking peep show booth. As they watch a gay adult film together, Perry lowers to the stranger's knees with the intention of giving oral sex, and the killer grabs a knife and stabs him in the back as the black-and-white porn film continues playing. The most vile and predatory side of the male dominant inclination turns into action, and blood stains this internal, hormone-driven oasis.

The bleak corridors of the police station and its empty and disquieting interrogation room; the cold marble slabs of the morgue; the isolated urban corners in which Steve Burns and Captain Edelson meet and exchange information; Hotel St. James on 109 West 45th Street where we witness the first and most articulated murder; Burns' rundown apartment and the neighbouring one of Ted Bailey and his boyfriend Gregory; the club scene on West Street, between West 10th Street and Christopher Street. It doesn't matter what the location or context is: the New York of Cruising is one in which Friedkin is attentive in keeping women relegated to the farthest corners of the backdrop. All the fleeting characterizations that are an integral part of the creation of context and a fundamental part of the filmic language and grammar are dedicated to men. Of course women can, on occasion, be noticed in the background, but the camera

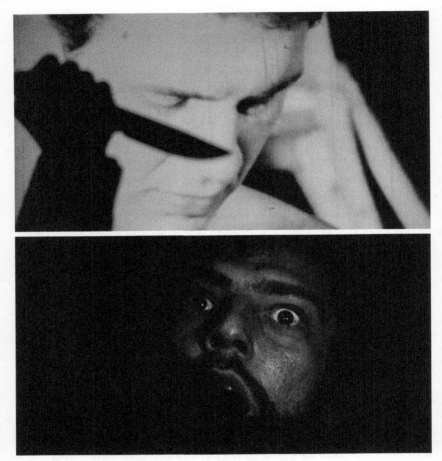

Martino Perry is killed in the peep show (© Lorimar/Warner Bros.)

never closes in on a face, never lingers on a shot which includes a female presence—not a waitress, a receptionist, a shop assistant, a nurse, a client in some café. Femininity is an abstract concept, one that fluctuates in the atmosphere but is essentially ignored by the protagonists: it lives in the over-the-top gestures and poses of the cross-dresser DaVinci played by Gene Davis; in the two strange, eerie-looking, crucified mannequins placed in Martino's shop window. Friedkin zooms his lens as if it were a microscope, and the female presence flutters on the borders attracting little to no attention. In fact, the first woman to appear on screen does so at 00:17:57 into the film, and after several different locations and night shots of sidewalks bustling with men, as if in some distorted sci-fi scenario of an old *Twilight Zone* episode.

The removal of the female element from the urban landscape is instrumental in amplifying the presence of the only real female character in the film, Nancy. Nancy is played by actress Karen Allen and appears, as previously mentioned, nearly twenty minutes into the film. It is unsurprising that her introduction is made with a frame-filling close-up, because she isn't just *a* woman, she is *the* woman: the only possible female in a world such as the one of *Cruising*. We know nothing about her: no backstory; no references to her job, daily life, or family; even the relationship that ties her to Steve Burns is never fleshed out for us. Have the two been dating for long? Is she his high school sweetheart? Do they have an exclusive relationship? Are they planning to get married, to build a family together? None of these answers is important. *Cruising* is an essential film: practical, and as visually rich and layered as the script is minimalist. Consistent with the style of Friedkin's best work, everything serves a purpose, and Nancy serves that of a conceptual function. It is important to note that she is never shown, except for a very brief moment in which we see her entering her condominium complex, in the outside world. She is always only ever in her own apartment and interacts with no one other than her alienated partner, not even on the phone. Her existence is inextricably tied to that of Steve Burns. Somebody could have fun theorizing that, similarly to Stuart Richards' father, Nancy is a figment of Steve's imagination, the physical manifestation of his heterosexual needs—a soft, accommodating, and understanding, motherly woman who waits patiently for him, and reassures him of his sexual inclination. As much as this theory has absolutely no foundation, and we could easily categorize it as cinephile masturbation, it would make for an interesting reading of the last scene of the film. While Burns is shaving in the bathroom, Nancy puts on his mirrored glasses and leather hat. The last pure thing in his life is contaminated and as the massive glasses hide Karen Allen's delicate features, Pacino's dead eyes turn towards us: now the metamorphosis is complete and irreversible. If she doesn't exist and is just a visual manifestation of his mind, then we are witnessing a change in that fraction of his psyche.

Karen Allen as Nancy (© Lorimar/Warner Bros.)

If we choose to take for granted that Burns is responsible for his neighbour Ted's brutal murder, then this can easily be considered a pivotal part of the last painful stage of his mutation. Don Scardino's character is undoubtedly a striking presence within the plethora of masculine figures that animate the world of *Cruising*: blonde, talkative, sensitive, and most importantly lacking an obvious strong sexual drive. Ted's talking about theatre, his career (or lack thereof), his joking about Shelley Winters' weight, and even more so his preoccupation with the mysterious murders that are terrorizing the gay leather scene as something removed from his everyday life make him an alien presence. He knows about what is going on but only through the news and papers as someone outside the scene would, making him, other than Nancy, the only character that doesn't live within the folds of the core narrative of the film. Ted is representative of the silent majority of the gay community in the film, but Friedkin's will to visually remove him from the macrocosm of men around which the film revolves pushes us to further question his function, especially in light of his becoming Burns' victim. Ted, with his pale t-shirts, flip-flops, and shorts is the everyday ambassador of the open, urban gay lifestyle. Not a single element of his persona brings us back to chains and squeaky leather. Burns develops a genuine affection towards Ted, and we do believe him when he tells him that he wishes there was something he could do to help his financial situation. The palpable empathy between our lead and Ted makes the latter's death ever more brutal. While the purity represented by Nancy in his life has been contaminated, in killing Ted, Burns has completely removed the last real shred of hope from his life—the last truly pure human tie he has created, and one that is not connected to the Mineshaft or the police force. Here, Burns has passed the point of no return.

Besides Karen Allen, only three other actresses officially appear in *Cruising*, all of whom are extras: Penny Gumeny, in her only screen role together with the one in *Soapdish* (1991) by Michael Hoffman (again in a bit part); Linda Gray, a prolific voice actress since the early seventies; and finally native New Yorker Sylvia Gassel (credited as Sylvia Gassell). To this list we could add Kirsten Baker as an uncredited 'Jogger', who horror aficionados might remember as Terry in the first 1981 *Friday the 13th* sequel, *Friday the 13th Part 2*, directed by Steve Miner.

Karen Allen was born Karen Jane Allen, on 5 October 1951, in Naperville, Illinois, to Ruth Patricia and Carroll Thompson Allen. She grew up as one of three sisters. Her mother worked as a university professor while her father was an FBI agent. Due to her father's job, Allen moved around a lot with her family and she has often stated that they would hardly stay more than a year in one given place. She had not thought about a career in acting until she was in her early twenties. However, she did want to pursue fashion. She completed her high school graduation from DuVal High School in Maryland when she was 17 years old and following that she moved to New York

City and enrolled in the Fashion Institute of Technology to pursue art and design. She pinpoints the moment in which she chose to get into acting as while watching a Jerzy Grotowski theatre production in New York, and soon after began her training in drama. She later enrolled in the Lee Strasberg Theatre and Film Institute. Allen made her major film debut in 1978, in *National Lampoon's Animal House* by John Landis. Her next two film appearances were in *The Wanderers* by Philip Kaufman, in 1979, and *A Small Circle of Friends* by Rob Cohen in 1980. Her career-changing role came soon after *Cruising*, with the blockbuster hit *Raiders of the Lost Ark* (1981), directed by Steven Spielberg, in which she played the feisty heroine Marion Ravenwood and love interest of Indiana Jones (Harrison Ford). Allen won a Saturn Award for Best Actress for her performance. After a few minor films, including leading roles in the dramatic thriller, *Split Image* (1982), directed by Ted Kotcheff, and the Paris-set romantic drama, *Until September* (1984), directed by Richard Marquand, she co-starred with Jeff Bridges in John Carpenter's science-fiction film *Starman* (1984). Allen debuted on Broadway in the 1982 production *The Monday After The Miracle*. In 1983, she played the lead in the off-Broadway play *Extremities*, a physically demanding role about a woman who turns the tables on a would-be rapist. She often took breaks from movie roles to concentrate on stage acting; Allen appeared as Laura in the Paul Newman-directed film version of the Tennessee Williams play *The Glass Menagerie*, with John Malkovich and Joanne Woodward, in 1987. From the early nineties, despite some high-profile projects, Allen's career slowly comes to a halt, but many films of the previous prolific decade—mainly the above-mentioned ones of Spielberg, Landis, and Carpenter—have made her a cult favourite for a whole generation of cinemagoers. Most of Allen's roles are characterized by an accentuated femininity but at the same time a fierce independent streak: sweet yet strong. The role of Marion Ravenwood concocted by Spielberg (Allen reprises her role in 2008 in *Indiana Jones and the Kingdom of the Crystal Skull*) seems to form the template of many characters to follow. In *Cruising* however, and despite Allen's naturally inquisitive and intelligent look, these aspects are undoubtedly downplayed. We've mentioned the most obvious function of Nancy's role as it fits into the downward spiral of the film's lead—the home, the refuge, the safe haven. 'Don't let me lose you.' It is interesting to note that the detached, alienated look that Burns leaves us with at the end of the film in fact precedes his entrance into the Mineshaft. Just a few hours after Captain

Edelson first bestows the case on him, he is lying in bed with Nancy and will utter the words: 'there are many things you don't know about me,' as he stares into existential nothingness. As the two lie in bed, man and woman in a plastic pose, it is unclear to whom this statement is directed. Nancy has likely been part of a charade for longer than we can imagine, an unknowing tool for the increasingly fragile psyche of the man she chooses to sleep next to. This makes her just another victim of *Cruising*, which is made more devastating by the fact that Nancy is one of the only positive aspects of Burns' world. Even her big, tastefully furnished flat is antithetical to the other locations: clean, wholesome, and mostly sun-bathed (it might just as well be his, but it's never presented in this way and we never see him live in it).

As we've hinted at more than once previously, all the men in the film lead a double life, creating a consequent dual urban reality. If this is undoubtedly true for the fauna at the end of that ramp of stairs, it is equally so for all the members of the police force. Most of the men can be placed within these two realities: both male-dominated worlds, made of unique rules and uniforms; of specific lingo and meeting points; and exclusive areas of control. Nancy is at the crossroad of these two exclusive clubs—one of badges, the other of leather. Although ignorance can be bliss, it is exactly her trusting, candid nature, and her innocent unawareness that makes her the victim she is.

(E.E)

TOUGH SKIN, ROUGH LEATHER: THE FACES OF *CRUISING*

My films are who I am, or at least, they are what fascinates and obsesses me. (Friedkin 2013: 377)

William Friedkin's search for reality—or better still his attempt to bring to the screen a stylistic realism—has been tackled more than once within the pages of this volume, together with his anthropologically detached yet morbidly curious look at the behavioural patterns, rituals, and codes that pervade and shape the world-within-a-world which is *Cruising*'s Mineshaft. Keeping these elements in mind it is only obvious, and shouldn't come as a surprise, that beyond actors and people we can talk about 'fauna'. The underworld described by Friedkin, the cruising arena, is as recognizable for its faces and bodies as it is for the lights and shadows that animate and envelop it, for its neon intermittence and its smoky corners. If we go back to a previously presented parallelism and think for a moment of the film not as a crude reportage of a slice of New York's underbelly but as a dystopic, parallel universe; a post-apocalyptic society constructed on primal needs and body-based parameters; a world sectioned by tribes, then it is only obvious that most of the men that are a part of it share similar physical traits and characteristics. As previously noted, the dark and damp world the film presents has a levelling power. Once each character steps into it and goes down that ramp of stairs that leads to the Mineshaft, he is letting go of a whole dimension, of the recognizable mainstream social façade with all the loose and fractured fragments it contains, and with financial stature being the first and most crucial one.

It is important to realize that everything pertaining to *Cruising* has a double: its broken people and the lives they lead, the police force, the official sexual inclinations of its characters. Everything has a distorted shadow following it, so all social elements that vanish while entering the trickling night to cruise is replaced by a counterpart: clothing, language, priorities. Unlike the mainstream world, and as we imagine it would be in a tribe, a form of visual identification is not only natural but necessary. The underbelly of *Cruising* is a visual world; what (and who) you want must be easily and visually decodable. It is 'a world unto itself'. After all, this is how Captain Edelson describes what the freshly recruited Steve Burns is about to immerse himself in. But in being so it mirrors our society, while distorting its features. The leather subculture denotes practices and styles of dress organized around sexual activities that involve leather clothing, such as leather jackets, vests, boots, chaps, harnesses, and other items of a similar nature. This is the simply worded and straightforward definition of the 'leather scene'. But the act of wearing leather garments is one way—the most striking perhaps—in which the participants in this subculture self-consciously distinguish themselves from other mainstream sexual currents. Wearing black leather clothing is an erotic fashion that expresses heightened masculinity and the appropriation of sexual power. So, just by taking into account the most obvious traits of this underground current, there is a specific will to hide and isolate itself, in the creation of an invisible playground in the backyard of society. In short, the film could be read as a socio-anthropological essay on the juxtaposition of tribal rituals within urban society. That said, this is not the only narrative or conceptual mechanism the Mineshaft serves within the film.

The shadow-bound pulsating depths of the club are a tailor-made rabbit hole for our protagonist. Is Burns chosen for the job because he looks like the victims, or is he a stray sheep being led back to its flock? Who are the victims and who are the headsmen to begin with? It's obvious that Friedkin's intention is to blur every border as much as possible, and in doing so the Mineshaft also becomes a metaphysical 'game space': a sort of frightening, yet eerily seducing scenario for our protagonist and the men within it; a reflection of Burns' desires and inner turmoil, as if he were walking through a carnival hall of distorting mirrors. When Al Pacino is moving around, exploring the flesh labyrinth of the Mineshaft, he fits into its folds perfectly. Friedkin does nothing to make him stand out visually. Of course, narratively speaking that was Burns' mission to begin with: to infiltrate this underworld, to 'disappear', as Edelson puts it. But Friedkin undeniably works on a more subliminal level and places Burns within this substrate as if he were a missing piece in a puzzle. He looks like everyone within it, assimilating easily, and in doing so becomes both victim and executioner. After all, if he is chosen specifically because he looks like the victims, and the victims themselves are the killers, then, as Friedkin's game with his audiences would suggest, Burns must also be both. Because everyone is exactly that in the Mineshaft: whoever kills dies, anyone we identify as the killer ends up being slaughtered, and if we want to go back and interpret the film's finale once more, then the end of Burns' inner turmoil is the perfect union of victim and killer in one tormented soul. Because maybe to be able to fully accept the dark side of one's subconscious something has to die, has to be sacrificed. So, it is only natural that in analysing the men of the Mineshaft the word 'fauna' is a legitimate one, because we are talking about a specific species, relevant in both the visual and conceptual design of the film.

Don Scardino as Ted (top) and James Remar as Gregory (© Lorimar/Warner Bros.)

Keeping this in mind it is interesting to note the casting choices when it comes to the males pertaining to each reality of *Cruising*. Let's split the film into three dimensions:

the Mineshaft and all its periphery; the police with its station and emissaries scattered around the Big Apple; and finally, the 'normal' world—the cafés and sidewalks of daily life. Three male-dominated worlds in which the only figures that seem to stand out are two from the final dimension: Don Scardino's Ted Bailey and his boyfriend Gregory, played by James Remar, are strikingly different compared to any other man within the confines of the Mineshaft and the nightlife that surrounds it. They are younger, blonde, slimmer, hairless, and especially in Scardino's case more feminine: delicate in their features and behaviour. On the other hand, the men of the law and the members of the Mineshaft seem to be visually and conceptually two sides of the same coin—a concept that is made all the more evident when the club throws a cop-themed night, and which ironically sees Burns being excluded from.

The opening scene really drives this point home and fleshes out the sordid communicating bridge between the two worlds. As patrolmen DiSimone (Joe Spinell) and Desher (Mike Starr) ride in their police car through Brooklyn's Meatpacking District, the latter's deadpan eyes scan the streets overflowing with leather-clad men as he deems them 'all scumbags', while DiSimone, speaks—with a calm yet menacing tone, as if to himself—about his wife who has just left him after ten years of marriage. 'I'll get that bitch,' he says. Spinell was also in the opening scene of Martin Scorsese's seminal masterpiece *Taxi Driver* (1976), and while watching this scene it's difficult not to recall the image of Travis Bickle (Robert De Niro) driving through a red-light district observing the sidewalks full of prostitutes and pimps. It is during this pivotal sequence of the film that we hear his voice announcing 'one day a real rain will come and wash all the scum off the streets'. Another moment from *Taxi Driver* that seems to tap into what is going on in the above-mentioned scene from *Cruising* is when Bickle finds himself listening to a customer who vows to murder his own cheating wife. From the illusory safety of his cab Bickle may believe he is removed from the decay and social sicknesses that he observes, but he is, without realising it, very much a part of the disease for which he sees himself as cure. An obvious parallel is drawn with DiSimone and Desher, who subsequently arrest a couple of cross-dressing hustlers and take advantage of them sexually. 'How do you know they're cops?' Captain Edelson asks, frustrated, when one of the cross-dressers lodges a complaint. 'You know how many guys I arrested last year for impersonating a cop? There's more guys out there impersonating cops than there are actual cops.' Edelson's words make a subtler point than is first apparent, and indicate the ambiguity that Friedkin is using *Cruising* to explore, which subliminally crosses the thin blue line between cops and the world, in the film, they seem to despise. Just as Travis Bickle is ultimately not protected by his cab, neither are *Cruising*'s policemen protected by their badges. This fundamental ambiguity is embedded in the film's very title, given that *cruising* has a dual meaning and can equally refer to a police car on patrol, or to the search for casual sex. We will see Spinell more than once again during the film: in the Mineshaft; walking through the alleys of Central Park hoping to hook up with Burns; and then again just before the film's ending when Edelson, wearing a defeated expression, seems to finally put all the pieces of the puzzle together.

Joe Spinell and Mike Starr as patrol cops (© Lorimar/Warner Bros.)

Joe Spinell (born Joseph Spagnuolo, 28 October 1936–13 January 1989) couldn't have been a more perfect choice, having become in the collective mind not only a figure indissolubly tied to the city he was born and died in, New York, but also associated with its most sordid and morally corrupt areas. Spinell, who was an accomplished and profoundly talented character actor for both the big and small screen, as well as a stage and off-Broadway performer, is undeniably a night animal, cinematically speaking, that has managed to incarnate the melancholy, frustration, and at times erupting violence of the discarded and marginalized members of society. Although Spinell's filmography is diverse, including such films as the Italian sci-fi extravaganza *Scontri stellari oltre la terza dimensione* ('Starcrash', 1978) by Luigi Cozzi, it is impossible to disentangle him from the image of smoke rising from sidewalk grids, sticky-looking strip clubs, and the muck-filled asphalt of the most decadent and forgotten side of metropolitan life. Many of his roles in the 1970s, among which the one in *Cruising*, seem to have helped Spinell articulate and shape the cult favourite which is *Maniac* (1980), directed by William Lustig—the first film that sees him as the absolute lead and arguably the one he is best remembered for—and which has often been defined by Spinell himself as a true labour of love.

We can only imagine how different *Cruising* would have turned out if it had starred Richard Gere, Friedkin's first choice for Steve Burns, rather than an Academy Award-nominated star such as Al Pacino. It is a well-known fact that Gere had expressed a strong interest in the part, and that Friedkin had opened negotiations with the actor's agent, feeling that the future star of *An Officer and a Gentleman* (1982) would have infused the role with a stronger androgynous quality. Ironically, a week before *Cruising* hit theatres, Paul Schrader's *American Gigolo* (1980) was released starring Gere in a profoundly sexually ambiguous role. Hypotheses aside, Pacino and Paul Sorvino were, at the time, the only famous or well-known actors of *Cruising*, because Friedkin, as he had done more than once previously and will do again often in subsequent films—the perfect example being *To Live and Die in L.A.*, formed exclusively of up-and-coming talent—will prefer unknowns, carefully picked from the city context in which he will be shooting, and often from the theatre stage rather than through Hollywood agencies. So it's no surprise that a large slice of the film's cast is composed of actors active in various Broadway theatre companies, like Richard Cox (who had been nominated for a Tony Award for his work on the Broadway show *Platinum* just a few months before production for *Cruising* began), the previously mentioned Don Scardino, and prolific character actor Jay Acovone as Skip Lee, the young man who gets wrongfully 'fingered' by Steve Burns. Special mention goes to Gene Davis in the small but scene-stealing role of the cross-dresser DaVinci. Many will remember Eugene M. Davis—brother of actor Brad Davis, star of such films as *Midnight Express* (1978) and *Querelle* (1982)—in the Ted Bundy-inspired role of the psychotic serial killer in J. Lee Thompson's sleaze-fest, *10 to Midnight* (1983), starring Charles Bronson during his Cannon Films years.

As is often the case with Friedkin-directed films you can find more than one future star within *Cruising*. Worth mentioning are at least three names: Ed O'Neill (12 April 1946, Youngstown, Ohio), James Remar (31 December 1953, Boston, Massachusetts) and Powers Boothe (1 June 1948, Snyder, Texas–14 May 2017, Los Angeles, California). As far as O'Neill is concerned—who can be seen in a few scenes, often at Randy Jurgensen's side, playing Detective Schreiber—*Cruising* represents his debut on the big screen, credited as Edward and not with the diminutive he will later become famous with, thanks to such TV shows as *Married with Children* and the more recent *Modern Family*. Undeniably, more interesting roles were given to Remar and Boothe. The latter, in his second screen appearance after an equally fleeting role in *The Goodbye Girl* (1977) by Herbert Ross, can only be seen for a few seconds, credited as 'Hankie Salesman', but he is the vehicle through which some precious information—pertaining to the meaning of the coloured handkerchiefs that can be seen worn by many members of the Mineshaft—is given to the audience. Boothe will not have to wait long to be noticed considering he will reach national attention the same year *Cruising* is released in cinema theatres, playing Jim Jones in the CBS TV movie, *Guyana Tragedy: The Story of Jim Jones*. Boothe's version of the crazed cult leader receives critical acclaim, and *Time* magazine goes so far as defining his performance as 'extraordinary'. Boothe wins an Emmy Award for his role, beating out such veterans as Henry Fonda and Jason Robards. Boothe's first iconic role for the big screen will be in Walter Hill's landmark action thriller *Southern Comfort* (1981).

Ironically, Walter Hill will play a pivotal role in the career of another young *Cruising* talent, giving James Remar not only one of his first roles but the one he is most remembered for. In fact, despite a filmography of more than 170 titles, Remar is forever enshrined in pop culture iconography in another 'tribal', night-based, metropolitan reimagining—as one of the warriors in the homonymous film Walter Hill directed one year prior to Friedkin's *Cruising*. Apart from a cameo appearance in *The Long Riders* (1980), after the violent and sexually aggressive character of Ajax in the aforementioned comic-strip-based cult item, Hill will give Remar another central role as the murdering sociopath Albert Ganz in the box office hit *48 Hrs.* (1982).

Powers Boothe explains the handkerchief code (top) and Paul Sorvino as Captain Edelson (© Lorimar/Warner Bros.)

At the end of it all, however, the face that seems to incarnate so much of what *Cruising* is all about is that of Paul Sorvino. Paul Anthony Sorvino (13 April 1939, Bensonhurst, Brooklyn, New York) is probably most remembered for his role as mobster Paul Vario in Martin Scorsese's classic gangster film *Goodfellas* (1990), and for his portrayal of NYPD Sergeant Phil Cerreta in the long-running TV series *Law & Order*. One of the quintessential character actors of the 1980s and 1990s, Sorvino's career has been studded with members of the police force, but it's difficult to find anything that can even come close to his Captain Edelson in *Cruising*. Edelson is getting close to the end of his ride, a broken, tired man that's running on empty and seems to be going through the motions. Having his character limp is an excellent touch, making his defeated aura ever more poignant. His passive look seems to be communicating an awareness right from the beginning, as if he knows Burns is one of the 'strange frightened little men' he is talking about during one of their secret meetings. In many ways it's not a coincidence that Friedkin lingers on his face just before ending the film, because just as Burns has finally completed his transformation, Edelson himself has reached the final stage of his own personal downfall. One through defeat and the other mutation, in their own unique ways both Burns and Edelson smell of death, trapped in their respective personal, private hells.

(E.E.)

A FOREIGN BODY, A *CRUISING* STAR: AL PACINO AS STEVE BURNS

> That isn't supposed to matter, I think, because the movie is really supposed to be about Pacino's progressive involvement with the S&M subculture. And there is some implied evidence that by the end of the movie Pacino is moving toward a gay orientation and does not find S&M all that unspeakably out of the question. (Ebert 1980)

The only voyage of discovery consists not in seeing new landscapes but in the willingness to look upon them with new eyes. Paraphrasing the well-known aphorism by Marcel Proust we can begin to identify one of the main elements of *Cruising*, both from an iconographic and visual perspective, as well as a purely conceptual one. From the glassy sheet of normality which lightly waves in front of them, through its raising and progressive disappearance, and right to the end when they are naked and raw, exposing what was there all along beyond the translucence of a normalizing social veil, so much of what *Cruising* is about articulates itself in the lead's eyes. As in most of William Friedkin's films—definitely in his best work—the context the narrative takes place in, as previously mentioned, is researched, designed, and filmed with a socio-anthropological predisposition in the attempt to create a palpable, colourful, and multi-layered realism. But the heart and soul rests in the protagonist's perceptions, struggling as he can with his context, and in the attempt to overcome an interior crisis his parable will often mutate into a downward spiral.

Steve Burns is a passive character, despite being a cop working undercover and finding himself at the centre of a mystery, a thriller. Burns doesn't run, doesn't shoot, doesn't roll over the hoods of cars. Despite many shared characteristics—first and foremost a self-destructive streak bubbling beneath the surface—there is one glaring difference between Burns and Friedkin's previous, and subsequent, members of law enforcement, and it lies in how they interact with their situations. They all find issue with their functions in the folds of their institutional hierarchies and the decaying urban landscape that surrounds them, which often ends up mirroring their own inner turmoil and anguish, but *The French Connection*'s 'Popeye' Doyle and *To Live and Die in L.A.*'s Chance trigger a violent war with their respective roles and consequent restrictions: shouting, shooting, digging their hands into the aching guts of their world; ripping and clawing their way towards an ultimate goal that transcends the cases they are investigating. Burns, on the other hand, observes, watches, stares, roams through naked bodies glistening with neon-tinged sweat. Before managing to arrest Stuart Richards, the gay music student he has been following, in the darkness of Morningside Park, we never see Burns taking charge.

Ironically, the only time he does take the initiative he will suffer the consequences of his own grave miscalculation. Burns mistakenly compels the police to interrogate young waiter Skip Lee, who will turn out not only to be innocent, but will be intimidated and beaten by the police in the attempt to extort a confession from him: something that Burns will witness and be part of. Interesting to note that despite being a cop and having, of course, participated in the operation to apprehend Lee, while in that interrogation room he seems just as frightened and confused as the suspect he is sitting next to. This is a well-known trope of many crime thrillers—the undercover agent staging his own interrogation—but the uneasiness and genuine daze Burns appears to be experiencing is anomalous and works subliminally to convey to the audience the idea that Burns doesn't seem to be properly integrated. The feeling given to us is not that of a police officer working cooperatively with a team of colleagues, but of a man overwhelmed by circumstance.

Doyle and Chance, just to stick with the previously mentioned Friedkin icons, are fiery and confrontational with the system they are part of and expected to uphold, but they are perceived as cops with exceptional deductive abilities—they are criticized but also well-respected by some, whereas Burns is depicted as a foreign body within the system. We rarely see him interacting with other policemen. In fact, the audience gets to see him gazing and moving around the Mineshaft more than walking through the corridors and offices of the police station. 'You fingered him,' says Captain Edelson when he meets up with Burns shortly after Skip Lee's interrogation. 'I fingered him, but I didn't think anyone was going to go that far with him,' Burns answers. In another moment Edelson will be even more colourful, telling Burns, 'We're up to our ass in this.' As the narrative progresses, we notice a blending of the language of the police investigation with homoerotic lingo. This blurring of the line between the worlds seems carried out to create an even more oppressive, taunting, and overwhelming atmosphere for Burns.

Another element present in all films dealing with undercover operations is witnessing the protagonist lose track of which side he is working for. We could go so far as defining this as the key dramaturgic characteristic of all films that deal with this kind of plot. In *Cruising*, this plays out through Steve's confusion regarding his sexual identity. On the one hand he is introduced to us as a heterosexual man, seemingly well-integrated within society with a career and a loving girlfriend, struggling to find his way through the labyrinthine world of this unfamiliar queer subculture, but on the other hand he reveals himself to be a deeply repressed gay man who cannot hide from the lies he has most likely always been telling himself. This progressive transformation in his character reaches a point at which, caught between desire and denial, we question whether he himself might not in fact be the killer, or at least on the verge of developing dangerous sociopathic inclinations. Through all this, *Cruising* becomes a confrontational viewing, one that uncompromisingly challenges its audiences—mainly heterosexual males—in their perceptions of sexuality: first and foremost, their own. Friedkin, as his directorial modus operandi dictates, doesn't make things easy for his viewers, and his line-up of sexual practices and highly eroticized and excessively manly naked bodies push each audience member towards an instinctive gut reaction. Burns seems to shift through a range of contrasting feelings as the story unfolds, but where he rests within the spectrum of possible reactions and emotions is unclear right until the end. When, during the last minutes in the final sequence of the film, he tells his girlfriend Nancy, 'I'm back,' we can't help but wonder what exactly he has brought back with him, in his warm and bourgeois home, and most importantly what he has brought back within him.

'What I'm doing is affecting me': Steve Burns is a delicate, fragile character. We cross narrative paths with the previously mentioned policemen and detectives of Friedkin's crime world—though the same could be said of other characters brought onto the screen by the director, an example being Father Damien Karras—seconds before they reach their breaking point, and the world as they know it starts crumbling around them. In the case of Steve Burns things are different; he is a slow burning character, one that has been hiding for years, and his awakening is less an explosion and more a psychological, emotional implosion followed by a personality transition that reaches its apex as we see him stare coldly at his own reflection in the mirror, pondering what he has become. As previously mentioned within this book, it was originally Richard Gere who was signed for the lead role in *Cruising*, and who was apparently very excited about the project. 'I think he would have been wonderful,' says Friedkin during the audio commentary present in the latest Arrow Video edition of the film (a must-buy purchase, which includes both an older commentary track with Friedkin as well as a newly recorded one with film critic Mark Kermode), 'because he had a strange, ambiguous quality about him.' Pacino got hold of the script and decided he wanted the part, and as one of the biggest and most acclaimed actors at the time it was decided that the film would benefit from his star power and probably help dilute the easily predictable controversies to come. It turned out that Pacino was extremely uncomfortable during filming. 'He had never frequented that world, and it freaked him out throughout the whole film. If there's a note that appears to be fear in his performance, it was there for real.' Although he agrees that Pacino's nervousness benefits the character, Friedkin makes it very clear that he wishes he had gone with Gere. Despite Pacino not being Friedkin's first choice, a decision that seems to have been dictated more by production and marketing needs, it's difficult now to imagine anybody else in the role of Steve Burns, and not only because his face has now been seared into the collective mind starring in the dark corners of the Mineshaft. Most importantly, such as in the case of Gere, it is hard to picture how the more canonically good looking and undoubtedly, as Friedkin correctly points out in the aforementioned commentary, more androgynous actor would have blended so fluidly into the pulsating population of the gay leather scene. *Cruising* is a world composed of men wearing tank tops, spurs, and leather gear; an SM arena of clones and mirroring doubles, and to a lurid and emphatic degree Friedkin places his protagonist among physically similar and identically garbed men, as if he were a product from the same factory. In the creation and anthropological illustration of the film's specific queer aesthetic, what seems to disappear is the line that separates strategic camouflaging and the impression of belonging. When and how does Pacino's Steve Burns stop mimicking and become an organic member of the world he's supposed to explore? So much of the answer to this question lies in the overlapping similarities between Burns and the men that are brushing off on him in the underground world they all find themselves encapsulated in. Physiological aspects aside, *Cruising* seems to fit Al Pacino like a glove, and Steve Burns is perfect as a 'bridging' character, possessing so many of the fragilities and vulnerabilities of his previous characters, while simultaneously the ambiguities and darker shades of what is yet to come.

It is difficult to picture Alfredo James Pacino (25 April 1940) in the context in which he was born: the future star of The Godfather (1972) and Scarface (1983) has come a long way from the South Bronx of his childhood. He was born in the East Harlem neighbourhood of New York City to Italian-American parents, Rose and Salvatore Pacino. The couple divorce when he is little more than an infant, and Alfredo ends up being raised by his loving mother and grandparents, Kate and James Gerardi, Italian immigrants, originally from the infamously well-known Sicilian town, Corleone. During his teenage years Al Pacino, or 'Sonny' as he gets nicknamed by his neighbourhood friends, dreams of becoming a baseball player, but clearly manifests an undeniable inclination towards the performing arts—so much so that in junior high he gets voted the most likely to succeed, mainly in recognition of his acting abilities. His first contact, at New York's High School of Performing Arts, with the Stanislavsky method he will later embrace and be known for will not be a positive one, but the young Pacino would only make it through his sophomore year before the need for money surpassed any other desire. This is the beginning of a confused yet rich and educational period for the future superstar; in fact, Pacino will take on a number of jobs, among which janitor, supermarket clerk, moving man, shoe salesman and mail boy, to name just a few. This vast range of people, situations, and experiences accompany him as he matures the decision to audition for the Actors Studio, at the time under the complete control of Lee Strasberg. Rejected but undeterred, he enrolled in another acting school, the Herbert Berghof Studio, where he met the man who would become his mentor, Charlie Laughton. Laughton not only taught him to act and directed him in his first public play, but he also introduced him to poets and writers who would help forge Pacino's heightened artistic sensitivity. He would be accepted by Strasberg's Actors Studio four years later. Just by taking these few biographical elements into account, we can immediately appreciate where the two principal components of Pacino's approach and persona come from: the streetwise attitude and tough, confrontational New York savviness, and the sophisticated, literary rich, and Shakespeare-loving attitude of a complex artist. Al Pacino is the perfect combination of carnal and rarefied, instinct and sensibility.

It is in the 1960s that he begins, timidly or with a tinge of wariness, to take his first steps towards cinema. During the heart of the decade he is still performing comedy revues, often written by himself with equally young friends and colleagues in the crowded coffee houses of Greenwich Village, while he also acts in independently produced plays, typically in warehouses and basements. Pacino evolves into an actor's actor, one than not only deeply loves the craft he is increasingly learning to handle, but that has a profound respect for his fellow actors. With this in mind, it is not surprising that he seems to create a large circle of colleagues and friends, all of whom he helps by bringing them with him on his journey to the top. One example of these could be John Cazale, who acted alongside Pacino in three out of the five films he managed to make before his tragic and untimely death. Another is in fact one of the corrupt and ambiguous *Cruising* cops, the New York-born Joe Spinell, who also shared the screen with him in three films throughout the 1970s.

Slowly but surely, year after year, Pacino refines his acting techniques, and consequentially, critics and audiences of the theatre world start noticing him. Awards and lauds won't take long to arrive and in fact, in 1966, he receives his first recognition in an off-off-Broadway production of *Why is a Crooked Letter*. Two years later, he wins an Obie Award for Best Actor in an off-Broadway production of *The Indian Wants the Bronx*. The following year, 1969, he is awarded his first Tony for his Broadway performance in *Does a Tiger Wear a Necktie?* Not surprisingly, that same year Pacino gets cast in the bittersweet comedy *Me, Natalie*, directed by Fred Coe and starring Patty Duke, James Farentino, Elsa Lanchester, and Martin Balsam. The story revolves around a young woman who moves to Greenwich Village, and the subsequent relationships and hardships she must live through. Pacino's small but significant role in the film will mark a pivotal turning point in his career, being definitively and irremediably lured by Hollywood's limelight. Besides Laughton, another decisive presence in Pacino's artistic history is Martin Bregman. Bregman managed by the early 1970s to become one of Hollywood's leading agents boasting, among others, such clients as Faye Dunaway, Woody Allen, Barbra Streisand, Bette Midler, and the future face of Steve Burns. Bregman will also help produce some of the actor's most significant films, *Serpico, Dog Day Afternoon*, and *Scarface*, and will help him land his first leading role in the underrated *The Panic in Needle Park* (1971), directed by Jerry Schatzberg. Rough and disturbing, this film is accentuated with an experimental vibe, telling the story of a New York drug addict named Bobby, and has only in more recent years picked up a very much deserved cult following. The protagonist of *Needle*

Park is the first social outcast in Pacino's gallery of portraits and encompasses many nuances that he will later elaborate on for subsequent characters. Bobby is intelligent, intuitive, and sensitive, though animated by what one could define as a social naivety: a self-destructive idealism that can't seem to find its place in society. Bobby is in a way a survivor, but lives on the peripheral branches of mainstream society, the dark arenas that are perceived as assaults on the American way of life: drug addicts, Italian Americans, gay people, homeless wanderers, or mafia members. Speaking of the last of these, it was a relative newcomer to the scene that gave Pacino the chance to be enshrined among the Hollywood heavyweights.

Francis Ford Coppola had great ambitions for the mafia epic he was preparing, *The Godfather*, and was determined to cast a virtually unknown talent in one of the key roles. After a long and intense negotiation with Paramount executives, who were opposed to both Pacino and to the faded Marlon Brando, perceived by them as non-bankable, Coppola finally manages to have his preferred father and son for the roles of Michael and Vito Corleone. As is well known, the film propels Al Pacino into the ranks of stardom and onto the pages of film history. The actor manages to infuse his performance with the spleen and angst that comes with mutation: the repression of one's spirit in order to motivate one's forceful willingness to change. Michael Corleone, with all the power at his disposal, is still a victim of his family, of his destiny, of his nature, and of circumstance. Pacino was nominated at the Academy Awards for Best Actor in a Supporting Role but did not attend the ceremony in protest of perceived category fraud, as his performance reflected greater screen time than that of his co-star Marlon Brando, who ended up winning the statuette as the lead.

For his third film, the now-established performer reunites with *Needle Park* director, Jerry Schatzberg, and another key performer of the 1970s and Friedkin star, Gene 'Popeye Doyle' Hackman. *Scarecrow* (1973) is another extreme examination of lives on the edge. Pacino and Hackman play two vagabonds, Max and Lionel, who, united by chance on the deserted paths of typical, bucolic, Americana landscapes, set off together in the pursuit of their respective dreams. Much of what characterizes the two is represented in the wide shots of the couple as they drift through the dusty roads of the country's heartland. Like the pairings in *Easy Rider* (1969) by Dennis Hopper and *Midnight Cowboy* (1969) by John Schlesinger, two other essential films that helped forged the cinematic evolution of the seventies, Max and Lionel come together out of desperation and social marginalization. Furthermore, Pacino's innocent yet intelligent and sensitive character seems to be the target of society's hate and violence, so much so that he will be the victim of rape, so costly to his personality that it takes only one more blow of fate to turn him into a catatonic schizophrenic. Despite the film's failure to deliver at the box office, the New York-born actor will dish out another superior performance in Sidney Lumet's *Serpico* (1973), in which he portrays the cop who exposed the corruption of the New York police force and put his life on the line in the process. Frank Serpico represents the first cop in Pacino's filmography and, ironically, despite being very different in spirit, will similarly to Steve Burns be alienated by his environment, becoming a foreign body within the system he is supposed to be a symbol of. This time he gets nominated for an Academy Award for Best Actor in a Leading Role, while his third nomination will arrive for the next step in the annihilation and dehumanizing revolution of now paterfamilias Michael Corleone in *The Godfather Part II* (1974): a controlled and troubling performance, which put the actor in a hospital bed due to exhaustion halfway through its making. The cold-blooded and calculating monster Michael has become in Coppola's second instalment of the crime saga amplifies and enriches his critique of blind capitalism and is an even more ferocious portrait of the tyranny of the American patriarchy. Pacino, interviewed by Andrew Yule for the book *Al Pacino: A Life on the Wire* (1991), comments on his character: 'There is such a dichotomy in Michael, he's so ambivalent. It's this dichotomy that finally leads to his madness. He is lost at the end. He's a beaten man.' Despite the difficulties the film entailed, once completed, Pacino will not wait long to sign up for another controversial and demanding yet memorable film, *Dog Day Afternoon* (1975), directed once more by Sidney Lumet. Like the previous *Serpico* and partly like the upcoming *Cruising*, this seminal chapter in seventies American cinema is based on true events, and like the two aforementioned Jerry Schatzberg films touches on the political anti-establishment vibe that permeated so strongly throughout the decade. Pacino's amateur bank robber, Sonny, becomes unwillingly or unknowingly a symbol of counterculture for the crowd pressing against the police blocks meters away from the bank entrance.

It is interesting to note that the star of *Cruising*, just five years previously, had starred in one of the first mainstream Hollywood films to tackle and include openly gay characters.

Dog Day Afternoon is naturally not the first attempt to bring queer themes to the big screen—we've mentioned in previous chapters William Friedkin's *The Boys in the Band* and in this one Schlesinger's *Midnight Cowboy*, which was slapped with an X rating precisely for the (homo)sexual overtones and implications of its story—but never had such a polarizing and beloved star, at the peak of his popularity, played an openly gay character. Further worthy of note is what had changed within Western culture between 1972, the year in which the real failed bank robbery occurred, and the year of the film's release. In fact, on 15 October 1973 the Australian and New Zealand College of Psychiatry Federal Council declares homosexuality not an illness—the first such body in the world to do so. In December of that same year the American Psychiatric Association removes homosexuality from its Diagnostic and Statistical Manual of Mental Disorders. During interviews, Lumet has often talked about the difficulties of finding an actor willing to accept the role, a man who backs himself into a corner in an attempt to find money for the sex reassignment surgery for his transgender partner Leon, and at the same time underlines the fearlessness with which Al Pacino applied himself in getting under Sonny's skin. In the documentary included in many DVD and Blu-ray editions of the film, Pacino talks about a moment that, though included in the script, never ended up being shot: when Leon and Sonny share a kiss in front of the eyes of police officers and bystanders. The reasoning behind the cut is explained by the actor as follows: 'When a relationship comes to an end, how often does sex come into it?' and adds that the ultimate goal was to portray 'the human conflict and the human cry for connection, and a kiss seemed to be exploitative'. Lumet, while also pointing out that the kiss did not occur in real life, adds that their relationship was based on 'two people who love each other and cannot find a way to live with each other'.

Contextualising in this way it becomes clear that Pacino had already gone through the process of decoding, analysing, and studying the way of portraying a gay man. When we find them, Sonny and Steve Burns exist on opposite sides of the same spectrum, though curiously they begin from a similar starting point. What seeps through about Sonny's backstory makes it clear that he had been living a socially and sexually typical lifestyle with a job and family—his wife and son—but Pacino, in a powerhouse performance, animates his character with subtle eccentricities and infuses the character with what we could define as an underdog's charm (the real John Wojtowicz on whom Sonny's character is based was also deployed in Vietnam). Sonny is a sympathetic loser: unsuccessful, broke, and as the film suggests surrounded by equally socially clumsy and marginalized friends. Steve Burns is, on the other hand, living in a highly masculine environment, the police force, a reality in which his sexual inclination would not only be noticed but would also isolate and 'finger' him as foreign body. The incompatibility Friedkin emphasizes subliminally would become tangible and real.

Despite Hollywood continuing to recognize his enormous talent, and his collecting accolades and praise, Pacino persisted in behaving very much like an outsider. He didn't move to Los Angeles but preferred to stay in his Manhattan apartment, systematically refusing interviews and defining himself principally a stage actor; to the theatre is where he will turn whenever he feels the need to withdraw from the pressure of his 'movie star' status, something he will do for quite some time after the release of *Dog Day Afternoon*. His next film is *Bobby Deerfield* (1977), the first of the two films that separate Pacino from *Cruising*, directed by Sydney Pollack. Pacino plays the titular role, a Formula One racer: a calculating, control-obsessed loner who, after witnessing a fiery crash that kills a teammate and seriously wounds a competitor, becomes unsettled by the spectre of death. His fear will find even deeper roots in him after his meeting with Lillian, played by Marthe Keller, an enigmatic and terminally ill woman he ends up falling in love with. The film didn't quite work for the public, and critics panned *Bobby Deerfield* as an over-the-top melodrama, defining its storyline clunky and pretentious, although many did reserve more generous words for Pacino's performance, which gained him a Golden Globe nomination for Best Actor in a Dramatic Role.

It is roughly around this time, in 1978, that Oliver Stone and iconic Vietnam veteran Ron Kovic begin working on a script based on the latter's autobiographical book, published two years prior, *Born on the Fourth of July*. As briefly mentioned in the first chapter of this book, one of the first directors attached to the project was William Friedkin, who had picked Al Pacino as the protagonist. Why Friedkin pulled out, or more likely was replaced by the producers is unclear, but what we do know is that TV specialist Daniel Petrie took his place for some time until the project was archived. The film was ultimately picked up again nearly ten years later, with Oliver Stone himself directing and starring Tom Cruise. Pacino will instead make *...And Justice for All* (1979) by Norman Jewison, which tells the story of an ethical lawyer fighting corruption within the judicial system. Jewison puts together a portrait piece, a cleverly conceived collage of situations that work perfectly as a stage for Pacino, who will, unsurprisingly, receive his fifth and last Oscar nomination of the decade. The nominations for the 1980 edition of the Academy Awards had not yet been announced when the actor was halfway through the production of *Cruising*. It is in precisely this thin slice of time that Pacino receives an on-set visit by 'Playboy' journalist Lawrence Grobel, waiting in his trailer at Waverly Place in Greenwich Village as Friedkin sets up the next scene. The result is a precious and rare interview—certainly the longest in Pacino's career. By this time the protests against the film have begun and it is clear from the interview that Pacino seems genuinely baffled and embarrassed by the gay community's reaction: 'I don't think the film is antigay, but I can only repeat—I'm responsible for giving the best performance I can. I took this role because the character is fascinating, a man who is ambiguous both morally and sexually; he's both an observer and a provocateur. It gave me an opportunity to paint a character impressionistically—a character who is something of a blur. I also took the role because Billy Friedkin is one of the best directors working today. My communication with the public is as an actor. Although I'd never want to do anything to harm the gay community—or the Italian-American community or the police community or *any* group I happen to represent onscreen—I can only respond in my capacity as an actor.'

(E.E.)

THE WANDERING DEMON: *CRUISING* AS A HORROR FILM

To me, it's just a murder mystery, with the gay leather scene as a backdrop. On another level it's about identity: do any of us really know who it is sitting next to us, or looking back at us in the mirror? (William Friedkin quoted in Simon 2007)

Steve Burns figuratively 'burns' in the crossfire of desires when he enters the 'infernal' world of the leather bars to serve as bait for a serial killer. As previously stated, in a number of scenes Friedkin suggests our protagonist is gradually finding himself more and more fascinated with the morbid world into which he is sent to explore, thus momentarily becoming an outsider to both that and the one that he occupied before. Friedkin deliberately creates a juxtaposition in two consecutive shots: with a clanking keychain, a steady walk, and a full leather outfit, Burns moves down a sidewalk and turns into an archway. After a hard cut, we see a man's hand, clasped in a black leather bracelet, clinging to the wooden bed frame, seeming to tug at the body with all its might—as if to intensify the power of penetration. Only a slow downward panning reveals that it's a love-making scene between Burns and his petite girlfriend. In this depiction, his overwhelming physical thrusts appear—complemented by her wide, almost absent eyes—almost aggressive: as if an attack on her subdued femininity, which has already been established in earlier scenes.

From the start, in complex, encrypted sequences Friedkin tells a cautionary tale of the narrow border between ritualized and destructive violence; at the beginning of the film, in a gruesome scene, a young gay man in a hotel room will be made defenceless as the killer brutally binds his arms behind his back. The 'psychodrama' of the sadomasochistic act flows seamlessly into a crime that is also punctured by Friedkin with short flashes of porn fragments (so-called subliminal images). 'You made me do that.' Before and after the short cut to the shades-covered face of the killer, who whispers this phrase in the voice of Stuart Richards' father, you can see close-ups of anal intercourse. In doing this, the film mixes sexually explicit and violent acts—penetration both during sex, and with a knife—and implies, problematically, that homosexuality is a sexual orientation associated with death. In its ambivalent presentation of sex between men, this montage also directly implements the 'Thanateros' implications of earlier films, such as *Un chant* d'amour (1950) by Jean Genet, and *Scorpio Rising* (1963) by Kenneth Anger. Like Rainer Werner Fassbinder later does in *Querelle* (1982), Friedkin also suggests with this collision montage (as established by Sergej Ėjzenštejn) that there is a connection between sexuality and violence: that they spring from the same primal instinct.

Steve Burns stabs Richards and finally confronts us directly (© Lorimar/Warner Bros.)

The serial-slasher that Burns eventually manages to uncover is repressed student Stuart Richards who is encouraged to commit murder by his imaginary, authoritarian father. Friedkin emphasizes an omniscient perspective throughout the film: he stages the encounter between Richards and his deceased father as an introspective break from the narrative flow in a contrasting, over-illuminated scene in a park. But this subjective perspective is woven into the narrative as subtly and ambiguously as the symbolism through which Friedkin narrates Burns' sexual transformation. Following this transformation and after the 'successful' conclusion of the case, Burns finds himself standing in front of his bathroom mirror, and it's at this point that the film reaches its pivotal narrative turning point. He shaves and washes his face but what he has lived through cannot be rinsed away. As Nancy discovers the clothing of his night-time 'alter ego', Burns' final look in the mirror suggests that he himself has inherited the personality of the killer. In the previous sequence another victim has been found while Richards is already in hospital recovering from the wound inflicted by Burns, and therefore under police surveillance. Captain Edelson seems to recognize the connection. What is subtext at first, now becomes clear: Cruising is a horror film hybrid. The killer instinct resembles a virus, a wandering demon that gradually takes possession of those involved—Pazuzu's demonic legacy from The Exorcist influences once again the American landscape. The loss of faith and trust that Friedkin's previous horror film diagnosed on a religious level is rooted in the heart of the big city. In a smooth cross-fade the film ends on the Hudson River, where a severed arm was first discovered right at the beginning of the film. Only now does the title appear, accompanied by Willy DeVille's low-key guitar chords.

In Cruising, which is generally considered a cop film and underestimated as a cryptic horror thriller, Friedkin uses the apocalyptic, 'modern primitive' charisma of the leather scene as an allegory: in darkened colours he visualizes the sexually bizarre as a subset of the patriarchal American society founded on violence. In a very open interview with Mark Kermode in Sight & Sound (1998), the heterosexual director himself acknowledges some of the fears that were expressed by the film's opponents: 'I understand their reaction, but I was not aware of the situation at the time we filmed, I did not think about what that might or might not say about the gay movement—I just used this subculture as the background to a murder story, plain and simple.' If you take a closer look at the murder sequences, the killer seems to shapeshift each time, often eventually becoming a victim himself (see Krohn 2004). The serial killer passes the 'virus' to someone else, in a fashion similar to that by which the entity in Gregory Hoblit's horror film Fallen (1998) possesses innocent bystanders, with each passage from host to host being underlined by the director with a particular song. With this in mind, the final scene leads us to believe that the virus has taken possession of Pacino's character. *Cruising* may not be the most obvious example of a horror film, but it's impossible to not see these elements growing more prevalent with each viewing of the film. The devil is clearly in the detail.

In the audio commentary for the DVD of *The Exorcist*, Friedkin says that he had deliberately kept the film 'styleless' in order to lend the frightening events a documentary effect that gave it its own authenticity. For *Cruising*, this thesis is superficial. *Cruising* is a provocative allegory, which dispenses its most controversial aspects subtly, especially if one chooses to read it as a commentary on gay sadomasochism: from the beginning, this subculture—itself of course only a small section of the gay community—seems obsessed with death; anal penetration leads directly to violence and destruction. Whereas Jean Genet brings a melancholic yearning into his cinematic poem, *Cruising* depicts a cold, infertile, male-oriented sexuality associated with death, the agony of a world without women, and 'the rectum as a grave' (Bersani 2009).

(M.S.)

BLACK LEATHER GLOVES: *CRUISING* AS A GLOBAL GIALLO

When I Close My Eyes I See Blood. (Lee 1980)

Stating that *Cruising* is a hybrid between an investigative drama and a horror film also hints at another possible perspective: William Friedkin's film could be regarded a 'global giallo'—an international variation of the typical Italian psychosexual thrillers of the 1970s (Stiglegger 2018, pp. 133–144). 'Giallo' in Italian simply means 'yellow'. The now familiar term derives from a yellow-coloured book series launched by the publishing house Mondadori in Milan in 1929, and the purpose of which was to provide Italian translations of mystery novels largely (though not exclusively) written by British and American authors, such as Agatha Christie, Arthur Conan Doyle, or Edgar Allan Poe. Previously, such mystery or detective stories in Italy were more a subgenre of the adventure narrative, but throughout the 1930s and 1940s the popularity of the imported genre grew. Mario Bava deserves the honour of having staged the prototype of the cinematic giallo in 1963 with his thriller *La ragazza che sapeva troppo* ('The Girl Who Knew Too Much'). The opening sequence can be regarded as a model for numerous later gialli up to Dario Argento's meta-reflexive *Tenebre* ('Tenebrae' 1982). The protagonist of the film, Nora (Letícia Román), is reading a classic giallo book on the plane when she arrives in Rome. In his article 'Playing with Genre', Gary Needham emphasizes that several key elements of the filmic giallo come together here: the self-reflection of the genre with regard to the well-publicized literary sources; the arrival of a stranger in Italy (the motif of travel and of the economic importance of tourism in Italy); and of course Rome as the main location of the giallo. Another important motif, which appears here for the first time, is the mentally unstable or even schizophrenic heroine, who does not clearly remember one essential element of her experience and must laboriously reconstruct it: did Nora truly witness a murder, or did she hallucinate? A mysterious doctor (John Saxon) seems to want to help but turns out to be just as deceptive as all the events unfolding around her. The quintessential tag line 'nothing is as it seems'—most importantly mentioned in Nicolas Roeg's *Don't Look Now* (1973), which was shot in Venice and can also be read as a global giallo—within the giallo genre will be imbued with new meaning. In this regard, the dramaturgic deception of Bava's proves to be trendsetting: in their private investigation into a series of murders, Nora and the doctor encounter a mentally confused murderess. It turns out that Nora did not remember the victimized woman, but the attacking offender. The famous black raincoat as a sign of the culprit or the perpetrator in giallo came from the fashion of the early sixties and was suitable as a unisex garment, effectively hiding the identity of the offender. This visual and narrative element only lasted throughout the seventies with few exceptions after, examples being some of Dario Argento's efforts of the following decade such as *Tenebre* and *Opera* ('Terror at the Opera', 1987).

Based on Mario Bava's *La ragazza che sapeva troppo*, which was released in the US as 'Evil Eye' with additional comedic scenes, a list of basic giallo motifs can be compiled:

1. The protagonist is at first innocently involved in a crime; their being an eyewitness is important and must be questioned and verified.

2. Some unknown element needs to be elucidated, often with a vague memory or mysterious dream serving as a clue.

3. The murderer is not necessarily to be found among the core characters, and is often female.

4. The killings are carried out according to a pattern or scheme intended to distract from the actual psychological motivations of the murderer.

5. The murders are stylized as dramaturgic highlights and often occur in gloomy or bizarre places (such as an art gallery or in a decidedly modern ambience); not infrequently the acts of violence are sexualized and carried out with phallic, slash-and-stab style weapons.

6. The offender wears a coat, headgear, and black leather gloves.

7. The protagonist is often a foreigner and comes to Italy as a tourist; this circumstance allowed directors to engage cash-effective international performers.

8. The motivation of the offender is often delivered in a flashback to a traumatic experience; sometimes these visionary retrospectives provide a backdrop for avant-garde dream sequences. The character design of the offender in a giallo often derives from a sometimes naïve or oversimplified psychoanalytic concept.

More clearly than many of his successors, Mario Bava works in his gialli with a glaring colour scheme, both in terms of the staging of objects that seem to lead a life of their own, and in the lighting, which creates extremely artificial spaces. The murder scenes, under Bava's eccentric direction, lead to dramatic set pieces that celebrate the state-of-the-art of creative killing. The astonishing longevity of the giallo is undeniable, with its formula still appearing in Dario Argento's more recent films, such as *Non ho sonno* ('Sleepless', 2001) and *Il cartaio* ('The Card Player', 2004), and even in some Japanese anime (an example being Satoshi Kon's *Perfect Blue* (1997)). Subsequently, Gary Needham (2003: 160) views giallo as not just an Italian genre, but rather as a 'discourse': 'something constructed out of various associations, networks, tensions and articulations of Italian cinema's textual and industrial specificity in the post-war period.' The giallo, then and now, employs: murder, investigation, strangeness, traumatized sexuality, and tourism, all of which are as key to other cultures as to the Italian. Therein lies the continuing relevance of this phenomenon, and the possibility of adopting its style and key elements for other cinematic traditions.

Ted's aesthetic death posture in Cruising *(© Lorimar/Warner Bros.)*

The international reception of cinematic giallo, which began in the late 1960s—also in the US—led to a mutual influence, which may be named retrospectively with the term 'global giallo'. The sexualized murder stories were designed from the beginning with an international audience in mind, and it is hardly surprising that their highly formalized degree of aestheticization has influenced some renowned directors. While Italian giallo was mainly produced between 1963 and 1982, its effects on world cinema can be observed from about 1965 to the present day. Above all, stylistic devices such as wide-screen compositions, dynamic camera shots, extreme close-ups of eyes, the fetishization of certain objects (razors, shoes), sexualized and aesthetic violence, expressive colours, and sometimes experimental soundtracks appear in numerous international productions, including the films of Brian De Palma, Quentin Tarantino, Hélène Cattet and Bruno Forzani, Andreas Marschall, and William Friedkin. From the beginning, giallo can be seen as a very self-confident and self-reflective cinema that uses cinematic means to think about cinema itself. In this process, rituals of seduction are played out—between the actors as well as between the screen and the audience. These mechanisms are cinematically exhibited, so that the audience must explicitly consider themselves part of this game of seduction. Like the later giallo-influenced films, the initial Italian gialli can be subdivided into various types: the erotic thriller; the investigative-based cop thriller; and the 'giallo fantastico'—the giallo and the horror film mix (Koven 2006). Often, investigative acts and sexual violence are mixed.

I would like to suggest the term 'global giallo' as a label for the non-Italian, giallo-style thriller. These international films have the stylistic peculiarities and substantive motifs of the classic Italian giallo or are at least strongly inspired by and reflective of these elements. Internationally, these include: the 'retro giallo', which is staged in classic Italian style, such as the German *Masks* (2011) by Andreas Marschall; and the 'meta giallo', which reflects the classical mechanisms while exhibiting the style itself, of which the Belgian *Amer* (2009) is a good example.

In Italian cinema, there is no term for the serial killer, although in fact it is in most gialli that a serial killer appears. While only metaphorical paraphrases (such as *il mostro*) exist in Italy, the serial killer movie is a well-established subgenre of the thriller in the US. So, there are strong reciprocal influences in this area between Italian gialli and international works such as Alfred Hitchcock's *Frenzy* (1972), John Carpenter's *Halloween* (1978), Sean S. Cunningham's *Friday the 13th* (1980), William Lustig's *Maniac* (1980), and William Friedkin's *Cruising*. To show how *Cruising* relates to Italian giallo, all the defining points above can be applied to Friedkin's film:

1. The protagonist is innocently involved in a crime by being sent into the subculture as bait for the killer. Here he becomes an eyewitness, collecting information and observations, but finally becoming a threat himself—a possible suspect for the last murder in the film.

2. The unknown element that needs to be identified and elucidated is the phenomenon of the 'wandering demon', as Friedkin only officially connects one murder with the prime suspect, Stuart Richards (the one in the porn cinema). The 'father dream' serves as a psychoanalytical key for the wandering demon.

3. The murderer is not necessarily to be found among the core characters, for most people acting in the subculture are only briefly introduced if at all—in some scenes we only hear the killer's voice, which is in fact the voice of Stuart Richards' dead father. Meanwhile, some protagonists in *Cruising* are ambivalent about their own sexuality or gender.

4. The killings are done according to a certain pattern, led by the key sentence from the dream sequence: 'You know what you have to do.'

5. The murder sequences in *Cruising* are stylized as dramaturgic highlights and often occur in bizarre or sexualized places like Central Park, a cheap hotel, or a porn theatre, and the acts of violence here are clearly sexualized, being carried out with phallic slash-and-stab weapons.

6. The offender masquerades by means of the 'black leather uniform' (well known in the BLUF (Breeches and Leather Uniform Fanclub) underground), headgear (a peaked leather cap), and eventually black leather gloves and aviator shades.

7. The protagonist is a newcomer to Manhattan's 'underbelly'—the Meatpacking District, 42nd Street sex cinemas, and the Central Park cruising area. Friedkin strategically casts an internationally well-known actor who is not associated with either this 'scene' or highly controversial material to act as a figure with whom the likewise 'inexperienced' audience can identify.

8. The motivation of the killer is clearly delivered in a traumatic experience from the past: Stuart Richards is hated by his father and acts out his consequent self-hatred by destroying other people. The surreal father–son scene serves as a visionary

retrospective to provide a backdrop for the simplified psychoanalytic tendency in character design. Yet Friedkin—who is not, in reality, psychoanalytically-inspired like Alfred Hitchcock or Dario Argento—does not rely on this scene and places many more alternate tracks.

With these points in mind, *Cruising* can be considered a prime example of a global giallo. Friedkin has never made a secret of his love for Italian cinema and his deep appreciation of Dario Argento's films of the 1970s, so maybe it is unsurprising how striking the similarities are between these and *Cruising*, though the director himself has never explicitly stated the influence the former had on the latter. Regardless, the shared elements between the two make a good argument for the idea of the giallo as a 'discourse' (Koven 2006), or a modus operandi at that time.

(M.S.)

THE CULT FILM: *CRUISING*'S HERITAGE AND LEGACY

> I loved *Cruising*—while everyone else was furiously condemning it. It had an underground decadence that wasn't that different from *The Story of O* or other European high porn of the 1960s. (Camille Paglia quoted in Adnum 2006)

In 1968 John Schlesinger had already caused a sensation with his melodrama *Midnight Cowboy*, which not only addressed male prostitution but also homosexuality, which had long been taboo in Hollywood as a result of the Motion Picture Production Code. The film received an X rating, as did Robert Aldrich's lesbian drama *The Killing of Sister George* (1968). Friedkin's film *The Boys in the Band* (1970), on the other hand, dealt less drastically with the dark aspects of a crisis of sexuality than with an authentic, albeit temporally and spatially condensed portrait of the gay community in New York in the late 1960s. Since Friedkin's staging remains extremely close to the adapted play, it was less the explicit depiction of homosexuality that became a scandal than the radical inside view of a purely gay microcosm, which the author Mart Crowley had designed using nine characters celebrating a friend's birthday. The play had already caused a sensation in advance, especially since some of the actors were abandoned by their agents when they chose to participate in the project. The success confirmed not only the existence of a gay target audience, but also the need to give this audience an authentic expression of their lifestyle. Despite an evident influence of Tennessee Williams' work, the piece went out of fashion with the rise of the Gay Liberation Front and was considered cliché. Mart Crowley himself decided to produce the film version of *The Boys in the Band* with the ensemble of the stage performance.

The film depicts the birthday party of several gay men joined by an uninvited (heterosexual) guest and a gigolo booked as a birthday present. The celebration gradually escalates in a way that reveals the darkest aspects of the male psyche and leads to the nervous breakdown of one of the men, Michael. Michael, the host, struggles with alcoholism and, as a Catholic, is going through a profound crisis of faith. His lack of self-respect ignites the drama bit by bit. His former college roommate, Alan, comes over unannounced to speak with Michael about an important matter that is never known to the audience. Alan is married and heterosexual, but the staging suggests he's hiding a secret. The pockmarked and Jewish-born Harold, the 'birthday boy', on the other hand, seems to be at peace with his homosexuality. Emory, Donald, and the couple Hank and Larry complete a kaleidoscope of various gay identities, the latter clearly playing out the competing models of secret identity and monogamy versus outing and promiscuity. Bernard comes from the African community and must deal with some childhood trauma, which is also only hinted at. The young gigolo dressed up as a sort of Midnight Cowboy appears as a gift and causes conflict and confusion. Friedkin's direction emphatically appropriates the piece and avoids the possible stasis of a chamber play. Film music, on the other hand, is left out here, apart from diegetically-fitted popular songs. *The Boys in the Band* works with strong contrasts, physical sharpness, and intense, supersaturated colours, which are reminiscent of the colour compositions of the classic Hollywood melodrama (an example being the films of Douglas Sirk). William Friedkin repeatedly emphasizes that the character-oriented staging of the studio production *The Boys in the Band* was considerably more difficult and challenging than the action scenes of his subsequent genre films. Regarding his late thrillers *Bug* (2007), and *Killer Joe* (2011), it becomes clear that Friedkin's basis lies in the extreme condensation of dramatic chamber play situations, the origin of which can be found in the final breakdown from *The Boys in the Band*.

Although William Friedkin cannot be considered a queer film-maker, homosexuality and men's fraternities are a key element in his work: from the police officers of *The French Connection* and the priests of *The Exorcist*, to the truck drivers of *Sorcerer* and the homoerotically drawn cops of *To Live and Die in L.A.*, Friedkin returned more explicitly to the New York gay world in *Cruising*, but showed another side of it here— the sadomasochistic underground of the leather clubs. While his earlier film *The Boys in the Band* was still largely greeted as emancipatory, Friedkin was accused of homophobia while filming *Cruising*. Today, both films, which come from the beginning and the end of the New Hollywood era, have firmly established themselves in the canon of international queer cinema. For Friedkin himself—as he emphasizes in the audio commentary on the DVD—*The Boys in the Band* is less a melancholy film about the gay scene than about fundamental human problems. Since the film was created long before the HIV epidemic, the later AIDS shock that devastated the gay community is not discussed here, but if one researches the history of the actors it quickly becomes clear that almost all of them died of immune deficiency over the course of the 1980s, and this retrospectively makes the film an indirect document of the disease. These two titles make out the gay world as seen through the eyes of William Friedkin. Misinterpreted readings of one world characterized by diverse colours and moods, destined to be shunned each one in its own special way. On this note the story of *Cruising* reached a sad climax when the production submitted it to the Motion Picture Association of America (MPAA) for approval and it was given an X rating (adults only). Friedkin (1997) recalls that he took the film before the MPAA board nearly fifty times at a cost of $50,000, and deleted forty minutes of footage from the original cut before he got the desired R rating:

> Much of it had something to do with the fascination of Pacino's character with the club happening—you know it now, but what went missing are the real excesses. We had a real fist-fucking scene with your fist stuck in the abdomen, golden showers, these things. And, importantly, Pacino was gradually being watched. ... Another sequence that is lost is one of my personal favourite scenes: it was inspired by a real event, two policemen, called the 'Pussy-Posse'. ... One of them, played by Joe Spinell, says to his partner: 'Whoever wins this game, can spank the other with his baton.' Obviously Spinell wants to lose ... Spinell gets out of the car, pulls down his pants and spreads himself to the police car. His partner beats him and he screams, 'Harder, harder, make it harder!' Later, when his partner really takes him down, he begins to sing: 'I drive to Kansas City, Kansas City, here I come!' ... The censor was hysterical, a direct attack on authority.

It should once again be highlighted: the title is a play on words with a dual meaning— 'cruising' can both describe police officers on patrol and gay men searching for fast sex alike. This aspect of the term is alluded to in the opening sequence, where the same cops arrest, humiliate, and sexually assault two leather cross-dressers. The sexual domination game in such moments appears as a perverted continuation of the real police authority. The exaggerated virility of these men leads to a restless search for self-exaltation in the humiliation of others. In the search for the ultimate penetration, finally, the fisting—especially as shown in the photo, *Double Fist Fuck*, by Robert Mapplethorpe—is the last desirable sensation, and male dominance felt through and through (Fritscher 1994).

Despite its rising scandal and the extensive *a priori* opinions, Friedkin's film appeared to be a failure at the domestic box office as well as with the critics. All hopes that the negative press might disappear when the film would finally be shown were gone. In fear of further controversy, the distributor added a written disclaimer before the film that underlined that *Cruising* is not supposed to be a representation of the whole gay community. *Cruising* was premiered on 8 February 1980 in New York. Was the director surprised by the hostile reactions? Friedkin told Alex Simon for *Venice Magazine* in 1997:

> It did [surprise me] to a great extent. Really the gay community was split. There were people who did not want shown anything that would present the gay community in anything but a good light, because the struggle for gay rights was in its very early stages then (1980). And I could see where the leaders of a certain element of the community would find this abhorrent because it wasn't showing the image of gays that they were promoting. On the other hand, there were a great many gays who saw the film who knew and understood that world and felt it was honest to that. A few years ago it was re-released in San Francisco at the Roxy Theatre in a brand new print, and the same outlets who'd ripped the shit out of it fifteen years earlier, like *The Chronicle*, gave it four stars. It got glowing write-ups in the gay press and guys were saying 'This is how some of us were.' I never made the film to have anything to do with the gay community other than as a background for a murder mystery. It was not meant to be pro or con, gay rights, or gay anything. It was an exotic background that people, I knew, hadn't seen in a mainstream film. That's what intrigued me about it. I had never seen it, but heard about it and decided to go around to the various (gay) clubs and saw what was going on, said that this was incredible. ... And I made the film, which I think leaves a lot to be desired as a film. It was severely cut, some of the best stuff was cut out of it. It was compromised severely then. It should've gone out as an 'X' picture, but they couldn't.

As the director has pointed out on several occasions, all that was cut from the film had to do with the explicit sexual content, in particular regarding the fist-fucking. With each new medium onto which the film has been released, Friedkin took his chance to add changes and make 'corrections' to his work. The early VHS versions prove to be the most similar to the theatrical version. For the Warner DVD and the recent Arrow Blu-ray Friedkin changed the colour scheme of the film significantly. But there are more changes: in the first reworked cut for DVD there is a street scene in which Pacino walks by a car with the licence plate 'FFA' (Fist-Fuckers of America). There are plenty of pornographic films from that era that show the extreme body techniques of the Meatpacking District clubs—Robert Mapplethorpe has documented some of these in his photo art. Still, *Cruising* might be the best-known document of that era and its protagonists, many of whom died of HIV or the AIDS disease, both of which were unknown at the time. It was around that period that the well-known French philosopher Michel Foucault visited the gay clubs of San Francisco as 'the philosopher with a mask' (Miller 2000). He also later died of AIDS in 1984. The long-time unknown origin of the disease at the time erased a huge part of that generation's gay community. Only two years after *Cruising*, German auteur and film-maker Rainer Werner Fassbinder released what would be his last film, *Querelle*—based on the novel by Jean Genet—which is not unlike *Cruising* in its approach to all-male virility and sexuality. The film takes place in a gay male fetish realm vaguely located in the Brest Harbour area. Black leather uniforms and hard and fast sex adventures dominate the scene.

At the time, *Cruising* was a flop, taking only $19.8 million at the box office. It was even nominated for three Golden Raspberry Awards: Worst Film, Worst Director, and Worst Screenplay. Renowned film critic Roger Ebert for example gave it 2.5 stars out of 5 with

License plate with the code FFA 69 as seen in the DVD version (© Lorimar/Warner Bros.)

this final comment: 'the movie's final scene—Pacino's girlfriend puts on his leathers and clanks toward him as the screen fades to black—is a complete red herring. Amazing. Here's a movie that's well visualized, that does a riveting job of exploring an authentic subculture, that has a fairly high level of genuine suspense from beginning to end ... and that then seems to make a conscious decision not to declare itself on its central subject. What does Friedkin finally think his movie is about?' (Ebert 1980) What today is seen as a key quality of the film was back then perceived as an unwillingness to commit. Yet this open ending is quite typical of Friedkin's approach to genre cinema with ambivalent protagonists:

> My belief that that's really closer to the way the world is [is what draws me to darker subject matter and characters]. I can only deal with characters that I know and understand and I've found that most of the people I know and have met are a combination of a great many things. They're not all good and not all evil. There's evil in good men and good in evil men. Hitler was beloved of his inner circle, and of Eva Braun and of his dog, Blondie. There's photographs of Hitler with little German children, him just beaming at these beautiful little kids, and them looking up at him like he's this benevolent granddaddy. And it's Hitler! Even though the foundation of American films is based on good guys and bad guys, that's not my experience in life. Or in self-analysis. There are times when I know my own motives are low, base, self-serving and there's other times when I'm able to do things that are quite selfless and kind and helpful to others and warm. I have and we all have these forces, good and evil, constantly at war within us. And sometimes the war is lost badly for the forces of good. Like Jeffrey Dahmer, or (Andrew Cunanan) for the Versace murder. I don't believe that he was born evil. But there was a mother that loved him at one time when he was a little child. And I tend to see these things. I don't want to make the guy a hero, by any means, but my initial impulse when I hear someone has crossed the line and committed a violent act is sadness. Sadness at the loss to all of humanity. And I feel that same sadness when I lose that battle within myself. Why make a film about someone, unless you're going to reveal something about their humanity? (Simon 1997)

In some countries the film was launched with a huge promotional campaign (e.g. in Germany) and in others (like Australia) it resonated more with the audience, but the legacy of *Cruising* rests upon its initial reception. 20th Century Fox released the film on VHS in the US and in Germany in uncut 4:3 versions. The German dubbing made a significant change: in the original English version, Burns erroneously addresses his superior with 'Captain Edelsteen' and gets corrected; his name is 'Edelson'. The German dubbed version changed the name of the captain. Here Burns addresses him with 'Edelman' and receives the answer that his real name is 'Edelsteen'. Why this is remains a secret, though it could be to do with a lip-syncing problem during the dubbing. For nearly a decade *Cruising* was on the German index of 'adult-only' films. Later it was removed from there and was rated FSK 16. It is now shown uncut on German free television. In other countries like the UK, the VHS was visibly censored during the murder sequences. All the various VHS versions contained the previously mentioned disclaimer prior to the film, and it was this version (and subsequent TV screenings) that kept it in circulation. It remained well-known especially in the gay community and its BDSM and fetish branches. Similarly to the rising cult status of Tom of Finland's gay leather comics that had been circulating for decades, the film *Cruising* became synonymous with gay leather fetish sex (very similar to Genet and Fassbinder's *Querelle*). The world created in the film proved to be a fetish fantasy and the film might have also been useful as a step of initiation into the gay BDSM realm for newbies. Like Tom of Finland's drawings, the imagery of *Cruising* keeps the icon of the 'gay leatherman' alive. It is one of the inspirational sources for the international BLUF subculture: the 'Breeches and Leather Uniform Fanclub', as it is known today.

Another cult item connected with the reception of *Cruising* is its genuine US punk rock soundtrack: the vinyl LP has been circulating collectors' stores for four decades now and is especially known for the title song by Willy DeVille. Quentin Tarantino used this exact song for the introduction of the second half of his film *Death Proof* (2007). Album producer Jack Nitzsche—who had also created the sound design of *The Exorcist* previously—invited the punk rock band the Germs to his studio and recorded six songs for the film, of which only one, 'Lion's Share', was used. In the 2019 collector's edition 3-LP set of the soundtrack the whole session is documented. In 1983 the influential industrial rock band the Leather Nun paid homage to *Cruising* and its music with the explicit song 'F.F.A.', about a fist fucking romance in a dark room. Nicolas Winding Refn used this song to great effect in his series *Too Old to Die Young* (2019)—a very twisted late nod to *Cruising* and Refn's idol, Friedkin. The Gerald Walker novel the film is based on was published in a new paperback edition as a tie-in to the film, which is misleading, given the deviations made by Friedkin's work.

When the age of DVD dawned towards the mid-1990s, *Cruising* remained unreleased for quite some time. A VHS upscale circulated for some years until Warner Bros. finally released a 'deluxe edition' DVD in 2007. This version was not the ultimate extended and restored director's cut, but it was supervised by the director who included some scenes not previously incorporated in the original VHS release and also altered the whole colour scheme, giving it a bluish tint, while adding some digital visual effects to the club scenes (including the one in which Pacino takes poppers). Friedkin also recorded a director's commentary track and cut the disclaimer at the beginning. Two short documentaries, *The History of Cruising* and *Exorcising Cruising*, shed light on the film's history and the controversies that surrounded it. In 2019 a special edition Blu-ray with a restored print of the film was released by British company Arrow Video. Yet again Friedkin altered the colour scheme—while the detail and sharpness of the images improved, it still doesn't have the natural look of the theatrical version. The often-criticized digital effects during the dance scenes were basically erased, but there is still a digitally altered frame of flashing lights. While the Blu-ray is certainly the best version around, it still fails to restore the original theatrical experience.

Fake promotional clip for the Cruising *playset (© Lorimar/Warner Bros./RamJac/Sundance)*

Along with the distribution history of the film itself, it began a second life in other media. At Sundance Film Festival in 2014, a short promotional trailer appeared. In rough early eighties video aesthetics it begins with some scenes from the film, then, looking just like a genuine commercial from the decade, hilariously goes on to introduce a *Cruising*-themed children's 'electric playset from Ram Jac'. In stark and comical contrast to the highly sexualised leathermen in the previously seen clips from the film, two small boys appear playing with the car track, taking on the role of the 'hungry hunter' on the prowl for 'handsome strangers'. As their father understandably looks on in alarm, they use a remote to make eye contact using 'eye-lock', and check the corresponding 'hanky code' (thankfully the key used here lacks any explicit language), before the trailer ends with a 'cop' showing up, who turns out to be 'just some guy dressed like a cop'. To understand the humour of this short the audience must be aware of the cult surrounding the film and its iconography. Several uploads are on YouTube with tens of thousands of views suggesting that many people are familiar with this work.

Around the same time, film-makers James Franco and Travis Mathews released their docu-fiction *Interior. Leather Bar* (2013). Both authors appear as film-makers on a project similar to *Cruising*, with an attempt to recreate the lost forty minutes of the latter. The title refers to a location description from the original shooting script. Instead of reinventing the highly sexual encounters in the leather bars around 1980, the film focuses on the process of directing sexual tension between men on screen, discussing creative and ethical issues with the actors. It is a meta-film on the film-making process, very much from a millennial perspective. During the shoot Franco phoned Friedkin to ask him what was shown in the missing scenes, though as is well known the cut scenes were highly pornographic. Thus, Franco's attempt can be seen as a self-reflection as a film-maker but does not much add to the original *Cruising* controversy. Regardless, this film, along with our other examples, is evidence of how vivid, inspiring, and important *Cruising* still is today, in its fortieth year of existence.

(M.S.)

BIBLIOGRAPHY

Adnum, M (2006) 'Cruising with Camille: An Interview with Camille Paglia' [online]. *Bright Lights Film Journal*. Available from: https://brightlightsfilm.com/cruising-camille-interview-camille-paglia/

Bersani, L. (2009) *Is the Rectum a Grave?: And other essays*. Chicago: University of Chicago Press.

Biskind, P. (1998) *Easy Riders, Raging Bulls: How the Sex-Drugs-And-Rock 'N Roll Generation Saved Hollywood*. New York: Simon & Schuster.

Canby, V. (1970) 'The Boys in the Band'. *New York Times*

Chion, Michel (1999) *The Voice in Cinema*. Translated by C. Gorbman. New York: Columbia University Press.

Clagett, T. D. (1990): *William Friedkin: Films of Aberration, Obsession, and Reality*. North Carolina: McFarland.

Ebert, R. (1980) 'Cruising' [online]. *Roger Ebert*. [Viewed 4 October 2019]. Available from: https://www.rogerebert.com/reviews/cruising-1980

Friedkin, W. (2013) *The Friedkin Connection: A Memoir*. New York: HarperCollins.

Fritscher, J. (1994) *Mapplethorpe: Assault with a Deadly Camera*. New York: Hastings House.

Greven, D. (2013) *Psycho-Sexual: Male Desire in Hitchcock, De Palma, Scorsese, and Friedkin*. Austin: University of Texas.

Grobel, Lawrence (1979) 'Al Pacino: The Playboy Interview'. *Playboy*, December. Available from: https://scrapsfromtheloft.com/2018/02/16/al-pacino-playboy-interview-1979/

Gross, L. (1995) 'Whatever Happened to William Friedkin?'. *Sight & Sound*, 5(12), pp. 14–15.

Gunn, D. W. (2016) *Gay American Novels, 1870–1970: A Reader's Guide*. North Carolina: McFarland.

Kermode, M. (1998) 'Cruise Control'. *Sight & Sound*, 8 (11), pp. 22–24.

Koven, M. J. (2006) *La Dolce Morte: Vernacular Cinema and the Italian Giallo Film*. Lanham: Scarecrow Press.

Krohn, B. (2004) 'Friedkin Out' [online]. *Rouge*. [Viewed 13 March 2020]. Available from: http://rouge.com.au/3/friedkin.html

Lee, N. (2007) 'Gay Old Time' [online]. *Village Voice*. Available from: https://www.villagevoice.com/2007/08/28/gay-old-time/

Lee, P. (1980) *When I Close My Eyes I See Blood*. Lorimar Records.

Martin, A. (2018) 'Cruising' [online]. *Film Critic: Adrian Martin*. [Viewed 20 October 2019]. Available from: http://www.filmcritic.com.au/reviews/c/cruising.html

Miller, J. (2000) *The Passion of Michel Foucault*. Harvard University Press.

Needham, G. (2003) 'Playing with Genre: Defining the Italian Giallo'. In: S. J. Schneider, ed. *Fear Without Frontiers. Horror Cinema Across the Globe*. Godalming: FAB Press. pp. 135–160.

Newman, K. (1988) *Nightmare Movies: A Critical Guide to Contemporary Horror Films*. New York: Harmony Press.

Russo, V. (1987) *The Celluloid Closet: Homosexuality in the Movies*. Revised ed. New York: Harper & Row.

Schoell, W. (1988) *Stay Out of the Shower: The Shocker Film Phenomenon*. London: Robinson Publishing.

Segaloff, N. (1990) *Hurricane Billy: The Stormy Life and Films of William Friedkin*. New York: William Morrow.

Simon, A. (1997) 'William Friedkin: Auteur of the Dark'. *Venice Magazine*, August. Available from: http://thehollywoodinterview.blogspot.com/2008/01/cruising-with-billy.html

Simon, A. (2007) 'Cruising with Billy'. *Venice Magazine*, September. Available from: http://thehollywoodinterview.blogspot.com/2008/01/cruising-with-billy.html

Stiglegger, M. (2000) *Splitter im Gewebe. Filmemacher zwischen Autorenfilm und Mainstreamkino*. Mainz: Bender.

Stiglegger, M. (2006) *Ritual und Verführung. Schaulust, Spektakel und Sinnlichkeit im Film*. Berlin: Bertz + Fischer.

Stiglegger, M. (2018) *Grenzueberschreitungen*. Berlin: Martin Schmitz.

White, M. (2014) 'Cruising: Speed'. *Fangoria*, May, pp. 18–20.

White, M. (2014) 'Cruising: A Report from Detective Lefransky'. *Fangoria*, June, pp. 46–49.

Wood, R. (1986) *Hollywood from Vietnam to Reagan*. New York: Columbia University Press.

Yule, A. (1991) *Al Pacino: A Life on the Wire*. New York: D. I. Fine.

Printed and bound by CPI Group (UK) Ltd, Croydon, CR0 4YY

13/04/2025

14656571-0002